P9-CEY-971

Positively

Dangerous

Live Loud, Be Real,
Change the World

Positively Dangerous is indeed a dangerous book to read. Frank Mercadante brings together powerful stories, the Scriptures, and strategies in a positively dangerous combination that will leave the reader of any age ready to recommit to the ultimate adventure—extreme friendship with and faith in Jesus. With simple yet profound truths that are easy to read and, more importantly, difficult to dismiss, Positively Dangerous has informed and inspired my heart. It has challenged me to live as a more positively dangerous person! It will do the same for you!

—*Jesse Manibusan, musician, storyteller,*
perfectly imperfect friend of God

Positively **Dangerous**
Live Loud, Be Real, Change the World

Frank Mercadante

Saint Mary's Press
Winona, Minnesota

The publishing team included Laurie Delgatto and Barbara Murray, development editors; Paul Grass, FSC, copy editor and typesetter; Gabrielle Koenig, production editor; Andy Palmer, art director; Kimberly K. Sonnek, designer; manufacturing coordinated by the production services department of Saint Mary's Press.

The scriptural quotations contained herein are from the New Revised Standard Version of the Bible, Catholic Edition. Copyright © 1993 and 1989 by the Division of Christian Education of the National Council of the Churches of Christ in the United States of America. All rights reserved.

The acknowledgments continue on page 114.

Copyright © 2003 by Cultiration Ministries. All rights reserved. No part of this book may be reproduced by any means without the written permission of the publisher.

Printed in the United States of America

5025

ISBN 978-0-88489-790-3

Library of Congress Cataloging-in-Publication Data

Mercadante, Frank.
    Positively dangerous : live loud, be real, change the world / Frank Mercadante.
        p. cm.
Summary: A collection of profiles of people of faith that illustrate ways to share, nurture, and express faith and love for God and one another, with authenticity and integrity, while making the most of evangelistic opportunities. Includes bibliographical references.
ISBN 978-0-88489-790-3
    1. Teenagers—Religious life—Juvenile literature. 2. Teenagers—Conduct of life—Juvenile literature. [1. Teenagers—Religious life. 2. Conduct of life. 3. Christian life.] I. Title.
BV4531.3.M47 2003
248.8'3—dc21

                                                                    2003000676

Author's Acknowledgments

Like any work, this book would not have been possible without the input, support, and encouragement of many people. This book is not entirely my own, but rather I share it with many generous and supportive friends.

I am grateful to the entire "Epapharus" team, who so kindly and generously prayed for me during the writing of this book. I credit you for any good that may come from this work.

I want to express my gratitude also to John and Peg Showalter, who so graciously provided their Galena, Illinois, home for me to work in as I wrote this book. The Lord is so present in your home.

I want to thank Jennifer Kuhn, whose contribution to this book is invaluable. I appreciate your gifts more than you'll ever know. You have always made me a better writer.

I am also grateful to Laurie Delgatto and Barbara Murray of Saint Mary's Press. Your valuable insights made this a better work.

I also want to thank Michelle Kilbourne, who took care of all the details of the Cultivation Ministries office so that I might better focus on this work. Additionally, I am grateful to the entire staff for supporting this effort in many ways. Thanks also to Eric Groth, Diane Honeyman, Ela Milewska, Jenny Mular, and Casey Ross.

I also want to thank my children, Sarah, Michael, Rebekah, Angela, Deborah, and Daniel, for their unselfish and genuine support of this project. With five of you in your teenage years, your editorial support was invaluable.

Finally, I want to thank my wife, Diane, whose ever unnoticed and uncelebrated sacrifice of a sometimes-absent and often-distracted husband made this book possible. Without your active support of this project and this ministry as a whole, this book never would have been possible.

Dedication

I want to dedicate this book to my parents, Frank Sr. and Mary Mercadante, whose love and support have been a constant example to me. Your parental love has been nothing less than "positively dangerous."

Contents

Introduction

Beware! This book is dangerous—positively dangerous! The following pages may change your life. This book is *positively* dangerous because if you apply the message to your life, it's "dangerous." You can be "positive" of that.

Additionally, the following pages are positively dangerous for others because if you apply what's written, you will live your faith in such a real, vibrant, and loud way that those around you will be in danger of catching it. Positively dangerous believers live their faith in an infectious, contagious manner.

If there is ever a time for an epidemic of faith to spread across our country, that time is now. Our world is spiritually starving and desperate for the hope of the Gospel. Who can better accomplish this feat than young believers? God has used youth in many ways throughout the centuries. We easily forget that our Catholic Tradition is filled with childhood saints and adolescent martyrs who lived their faith with nothing less than heroism. Make no mistake about it—today's youth are capable of the same kind of world-changing impact. When young people apply their natural energy, enthusiasm, and idealism to living and spreading the Gospel, nothing can stand in their way. I hope you can use this book as a tool to this end in your life.

Positively Dangerous is not about hype as much as it is about depth. It's not about image as much as it is about substance. Dangerous persons of faith are able to extend the Kingdom of God to the world around them because such people have a living, vibrant, and deep relationship with Jesus Christ. Living loud isn't about raising the decibels of our words by out-shouting those around us. Words that ring with depth, even when uttered softly, will always rise above the shallow words of hype.

Becoming positively dangerous is not what you can *do* but what you can *be.* It's not about changing others as much as it is about changing yourself. You are the danger factor— your relationship with God and the way you conduct your life. Others are only vulnerable because you live and share your life in such a positive way that it becomes dangerously contagious.

Too often teens are offered "Christianity Lite," an expression of faith that tastes great on the surface but is less filling to the soul. Young people want more than that. Most teens want to make a difference in their world. They want to invest their life in a worthy adventure that has the potential to change their world. You have this book in your hands because you are the kind of teen God can use as a history changer.

You can read *Positively Dangerous* alone or use it in a group. Please take time to consider the questions for reflection and discussion at the end of each chapter. They are designed to help you integrate and apply the message of this book.

For the latest in becoming positively dangerous, visit the Cultivation Ministries Web site at *www.outbreak-of-faith.org.*

Chapter 1
You Dangerous!

David, a popular member of our peer ministry team, was
having a great junior year. He was a well-respected
leader, earned A's in school, and dated Nicole, a very
attractive senior peer minister. However, David was not
the only ministry team member interested in Nicole; so
was Steven. As a matter of fact, Steven repeatedly badg-
ered Nicole about her relationship with David. He didn't
think they were right for each other, and he wasn't timid
about sharing his opinion with David, Nicole, and anyone
else who'd listen. David laughed off Steven's competitive
remarks as jokes and his apparent attraction to Nicole as
no real threat—until she suddenly broke off their relationship. To make matters worse, before the ink dried on
David's "Dear John" letter, Steven asked Nicole to be his

date for their senior prom—and she accepted the invitation.

David didn't take this rebuff lightly. To say he was emotionally upset is a bit of an understatement. He felt he was in love with Nicole and was devastated by the breakup and the thought of her going hand in hand to the prom with that slimy, backstabbing Steven. His friends began to notice a change in David's disposition. He started to say and do things that were uncharacteristic of his personality. I figured he was only a novice in dealing with these new and intense feelings of love and was experiencing some emotional awkwardness. Others said it more starkly: "David has gone off the deep end!"

All three were on our peer ministry team, and before long the battle lines were drawn; everyone had an opinion on who was right or wrong in this teenage love triangle. Our team was falling apart, and I knew I had to intervene.

I gathered the three of them in my office in an attempt to facilitate some type of reconciliation and healing. As the meeting began, Steven and David exchanged verbal blows while Nicole, the object of their modern-day chivalry, sat awkwardly and in obvious discomfort. I mediated as best I could, repeatedly going two steps forward and three back, as the boys emotionally triggered each other. We were spared any uncontrolled shouting, but the personal, verbal jabs between David and Steven demonstrated the depths of their anger toward each other. As the heated discussion continued, the tension in the room mounted. Eventually, David said that he needed a break, and he asked to be excused for a moment to get something from his car. We all needed a breather, so I readily consented.

While David was gone, I started to wonder what he needed from his car. As my mind entertained all the possibilities, I kept trying to talk myself out of one crazy thought. David was obviously upset with Steven and emotionally devastated by the breakup. He had not been acting like himself lately, and I wondered what was running through his mind. I had read stories in the paper about similar incidents where people had resorted to violent acts. Was David capable of this? I did not think so—he was one of my finest students. On the other hand, he was pretty upset and was already acting strangely. Good people do snap, I thought. I was startled out of my daydream by David's returning to my office and shuffling to place an unknown object behind the door.

David then stood at the entrance, facing Steven, Nicole, and me. He did not proceed back to his chair but remained in the doorway, his hands behind his back. He was obviously concealing something! I swallowed hard as a jolt of adrenaline surged through my body. What is he hiding from us? I anxiously asked myself.

David began to address Steven with an introductory speech, the kind that precedes some type of momentous and memorable occasion—like the words people pronounce before giving an award, a wedding proposal, a prison sentence, or even an execution. In a nervous and quivering voice, David stated: "Steven, what you did to me was wrong, and I feel betrayed by you. You hurt me deeply by your negative words during the year, and now you've taken my girlfriend."

I craned my neck in a desperate attempt to catch a glimpse of what David held in his hands, but he had intentionally positioned himself so that no one could see what he was hiding. Steven and Nicole became visibly anxious, and I mentally prepared myself for the worst—in case David had concealed a knife or a gun behind his back. I was the closest to David, and as soon as I could identify a weapon in his hand, I was determined to pounce on him and save Steven from harm.

I will never forget what happened next. David finished his introductory speech and was about to initiate the action we all awaited. His hands started to move forward from behind his back. I visually locked in on his hands and moved into a position to tackle him. Sweat was dripping down my face as I was nearing my "life or death" cue. When I caught sight of what David was holding, my jaw dropped. He held a small, scrunched-up hand towel. He proceeded to reach behind my door for the container of water he had concealed there, brought it forward, and knelt at Steven's feet. He then said, "Steven, I forgive you and want to wash your feet as a gesture of my forgiveness and reconciliation." David took off Steven's shoes and socks and washed his feet. The three of us were stunned and silent. When David finished, he embraced Steven and reaffirmed his forgiveness and his desire to be reconciled.

(Adapted from Frank Mercadante,
Growing Teen Disciples, pp. 244–246)

David was one dangerous guy! But the situation did not (thank God) play out in the negative way I was anticipating. When David returned from his car, I sincerely believed he was concealing a weapon, and I considered him to be an extremely dangerous person. He seemingly had placed us all at risk, and I felt very unsafe. Fortunately, his "weapons" were a pitcher of water and a towel, wielded in love, which became instruments of healing rather than means of destruction. On that memorable day, I became the victim of David's living out his faith dangerously, and my life changed as a result.

Yes, David was dangerous, but he was *positively* dangerous. He had read the Gospel account where Jesus stoops to the ground in humility and, like the lowliest servant, washes the feet of Judas, a man about to betray him. But David hadn't just read the words as another nice Jesus story; instead, he had taken Jesus' words to heart (see John 13:14). David was serious about following Jesus. He reasoned, If that's what my Lord does with his "enemy," that's what I must do with my "enemy" to be a disciple of Christ. David's faith was real, and he actively applied it to his life's circumstances. His decision to follow Jesus instead of his bruised ego and wounded heart made him *positively* dangerous to all of us in that room and brought peace to a troubled peer ministry team.

We Are All Dangerous

Most people do not view themselves as dangerous. If someone told you, "You pose a dangerous threat to others," you would likely be offended. What does it mean to be dangerous? The dictionary defines *dangerous* as "unsafe, perilous, full of danger, exposed to possible risk, adventurous." Some forms of danger we fear; others attract us.

News shows and newspapers remind us of danger's negative presence in our daily life. We see danger's most unattractive side in school shootings, gang violence, drug and alcohol abuse, and terrorism.

Strangely enough, though, we are attracted to danger's adventurous side. A person involved in extreme sports is an example of someone who craves danger's excitement. Because Hollywood producers also know that audiences ache for the thrill of danger, they use it to drive many movies and television shows. Danger sells. We are somehow tantalized by the risk and adventure that danger offers.

Danger can be both compelling and repulsive, but our Catholic faith is not something we normally associate with either of these aspects of danger. Going to church on Sunday is not dangerous. Reading the Scriptures doesn't seem so dangerous, except for the occasional paper cuts we get when turning the pages. So what can be so dangerous about living our faith? The fact is that the way we live our faith not only places others at risk but also offers us a sense of adventure like nothing else in this world.

As unbelievable and even ironic as it may seem, *you* are already dangerous. Everyone who calls himself or herself Catholic or Christian is *already* dangerous. So the question isn't "Are we dangerous?" That's a given. The real question is "Are we positively dangerous or negatively dangerous?" Does the lively manner in which we live our faith place others at serious risk of catching our faith? Or does our lifeless, even contradictory, expression of faith give others a credible reason to reject our faith as irrelevant?

Two Types of Dangerous Faith

We can live our faith in two ways: positively or negatively. If we are in love with Jesus and allow our faith to affect our actions, we have a positively dangerous faith and put others at risk of personally encountering Jesus. But if we are not in a vibrant relationship with Christ, and if our faith doesn't affect how we act, we are negatively dangerous to others and can create barriers that prevent them from knowing Christ. The most dangerous threats to Christianity are *not* from the outside. The most significant menace is not from oppressive governments, terrorists, or skeptical atheists trying to disprove our faith. The most perilous threats usually originate from the inside—from us! The greatest challenge to Christianity is whether we, who profess to have faith in Christ, live out that faith in daily life.

Weak Strains of Faith

All of us have received some type of vaccination against childhood diseases, such as measles, polio, or hepatitis B. Vaccines introduce a weak strain of the virus into our system to build antibodies that resist the illness in case of future exposure. In turn, our body becomes immune to the disease.

The same process can happen when people are exposed to weak strains of Christianity. Unbelievers can encounter weak strains of faith and be turned off, whereupon they build resistance to God and to religion. Our own anemic expression of faith often immunizes others from catching it. These weak strains of faith, which cause other people to become resistant to God or to the Church, are examples of being negatively dangerous.

Two negatively dangerous strains of faith in particular can vaccinate others from catching the real thing. These two dangerous spiritual maladies are *apathy* and *hypocrisy*. If we are living our faith apathetically, lifelessly, and indifferently, our searching friends will look right past us because they won't see anything in our life that is different from their own. They may reason that Christianity doesn't make a difference in our life. Worse yet, our friends may dismiss Jesus and the Church because of our hypocrisy (saying one thing but doing another).

Let's take a closer look at each of these expressions of negatively dangerous faith.

Spiritual Apathy

Apathetic faith is indifferent and passionless Christianity: living our faith as if the "Good News" of the Gospel isn't all that good. It's "cottage-cheese Christianity." Like the dull flavor of cottage cheese, our expression of faith is bland, boring, and tasteless. No one takes a mouthful of cottage cheese and enthusiastically yells: "Wow! My taste buds are screaming in ecstasy!" Likewise, no one observes a person with apathetic faith and shouts: "Wow! Your faith is so compelling that I want what you have for myself!" Apathetic faith does nothing to attract people to Jesus. Instead, it subconsciously sends potential believers down divergent spiritual paths.

Unfortunately, an apathetic expression of faith is all too common among those of us who profess to believe. As a result we have lost many potential believers because of our own passionless faith. For example, the Indian leader Mahatma Gandhi was very interested in Christianity. While attending a university in London, he was fascinated by the person of Jesus and was nearly convinced that Christianity is a religion distinct from all others. Once graduated, Gandhi continued to consider converting to Christianity. While working in East Africa, he lived with a Christian family who attended church regularly. Gandhi figured this would provide the best evidence on whether the Christian faith is something worth devoting his life to.

Gandhi stayed with this family for seven months. Afterward, he concluded that Christianity is just one of many religions in the world. He became disillusioned by the spiritual apathy of Christians after watching them sleep through church services, hearing them complain about sacrificing for Christ, and witnessing them live their faith with little conviction or passion.

Jesus describes spiritual apathy as being "lukewarm." He says to the church of Laodicea: "I know your works; you are neither cold nor hot. I wish that you were either cold or hot. So, because you are lukewarm, and neither cold nor hot, I am about to spit you out of my mouth" (Revelation 3:15–16).

The word translated as *spit* literally means "to hurl, or to vomit"! Jesus' graphic image is less than flattering! He finds lukewarm, apathetic expressions of faith rather nauseating.

Spicy Faith

Following Jesus is never meant to be boring and bland like the flavor of cottage cheese. Rather, it should be positively explosive and spicy like the taste of jalapeÖo peppers! Taking a bite of a jalapeÖo is a memorable encounter. You don't soon forget it: spicy going in, hot going down, and burning going out! The Apostles live their faith like "jalapeÖo believers." The Book of Acts describes their positive impact as "turning the world upside down" (17:6).

Many people don't know how exciting, adventurous, and life impacting our faith is meant to be. I say this because I was one such teenager. I always believed God existed, but I thought God was distant, aloof, and uninterested in my life. I had no idea God could be so personal, so real, so willing to be an everyday part of my life. I lived an apathetic, cottage-cheese faith because I thought cottage cheese was the only option on the menu. I attended Mass on Sunday and scanned a filled sanctuary of fellow Mass-goers. Everyone looked miserable, as if suffering from constipation. I became accustomed and thought it was normal Christian living. No wonder I became a fifth-grade religious education dropout!

During my senior year, however, I awakened from my yawning, slumbering faith. I met some fellow students who lived differently. Their faith was real, alive, and fully integrated into their life. They talked as if Jesus was their close, personal friend. What they had was unique, different, and yet very attractive. I didn't realize it at the time, but I was searching for something more. As a result of their persistent invitation, I reluctantly attended a retreat they led, and my life has never been the same. For the first time, I opened the awesome gift of a relationship with Christ that was given to me at Baptism. I understood the difference between *knowing about* Jesus and *knowing* him. I met Jesus in such a personal and profound way that my life moved from black and white to living color.

I want you to know that Jesus' promise of "abundant life" (John 10:10) is not the empty promise of a shady telemarketer or just hollow words. His promise is the real deal, and Jesus so earnestly desires to give it to us that he is willing to suffer and die for each and every one of us. The life that God has for us is abundant and is the only life we are meant to experience.

Hypocrisy

We have seen how we, by living our faith apathetically, can be negatively dangerous and place others at risk of ignoring and rejecting it. A second expression of faith that is as lethally dangerous is hypocrisy, which literally means "playacting." We play the role of a hypocrite when we say one thing but do another, when we don't "walk the talk." A hypocrite is a dishonest person. Hypocrisy describes someone who portrays one thing but in reality is something else.

A Christian magazine once asked students at three Illinois colleges to explain why Christianity didn't appeal to them. From a list of eight reasons, the majority chose this response: "I've met too many Christians who are hypocritical." It is pretty sad when hypocrisy becomes synonymous with Christianity! Such an indictment is clear: nothing about the life of Christians is attractive and positively compelling; our life is a contradiction of what we Christians believe.

Following Jesus requires much more than attending church and casually assenting to the beliefs of the faith. Our actions should shout and scream to those around us what we truly believe. Saint Francis of Assisi lived and taught the ideal that we should preach the Gospel at all times and use words only when necessary. Our life should be a rich and compelling sermon that draws others to Jesus. Our actions should concretely illustrate the truths of the Gospel.

Hypocritical Christians are negatively dangerous and place those around them at serious risk of rejecting the validity of Jesus' message. We find an example of the negative impact of such hypocrisy in the story of one young man who grew up in a German Jewish family.

> This family, devout in its beliefs and customs and very involved in the Jewish community, later settled in another part of Germany. One day, the father came home and informed his family that they would no longer be attending the Jewish synagogue. They were now Lutheran, he announced, and they would go to the Lutheran church. When the young son, alarmed, asked for an explanation, his father replied that the change was for financial reasons. He would acquire more business contacts, and it would be more profitable for him to be a member of the Lutheran church.
>
> The young son was upset and bitter about his father's decision. When he grew up, he left Germany. While studying in England, he authored the well-known words, "Religion is the opiate of the people." He had concluded that religion is merely an escape from reality and that religious people are as misguided as those who take drugs. His atheistic approach to life has influenced the lives of millions of people. That young son, whose father's hypocrisy affected him so negatively, was Karl Marx, the founder of Marxism.
>
> (Adapted from Cliffe Knechtle, *Give Me an Answer,* p. 95)

Called to Be a Positive Example

The Apostle Paul is clear about the importance of our life's being a positive example to others. He sets the standard high when he tells other believers to imitate him as he imitates

Christ (see 1 Corinthians 11:1). Also, he tells the young leader Timothy, "Let no one despise your youth, but set the believers an example in speech and conduct, in love, in faith, in purity" (1 Timothy 4:12). The Greek word Paul uses that we translate as "example" is *tupos,* from which we get the word *type.* Paul calls us to live as a type, or standard, that accurately illustrates the truth of the Gospel. The Greek word *tupos* also carries the connotation, or idea, of a mark that results from a blow, like a hand imprint after a slap. Paul is saying that our life should leave an imprint, a mark, upon all those we meet. We should leave behind an indelible reminder on all those around us of what it means to follow Jesus.

Two Types of Hypocrisy

Hypocrisy, although certainly not attractive, is present to one degree or another in everyone's life. To deny its presence makes us the most dangerous of hypocrites. The Pharisees are prime examples of this attitude. Jesus reserves his harshest words for the Pharisees, calling them "blind guides and hypocrites" (Matthew 23:15–16,23–24) because they think of themselves as being the most holy of men while they are wholly fake.

There will always be a gap between what we believe and how we live those beliefs in our life. It's my experience that the Lord's love and mercy allow us to see only a little bit of our hypocrisy at a time. To see it in its ugly entirety would prove to be too overwhelming for any one person.

Because hypocrisy is present in everyone's life, we can either humbly admit our hypocrisy and draw closer to Jesus, or we can deny it through pride and separate ourselves from him. Humility gives us clear vision; pride blinds us from our true condition. Humility helps us recognize our need for God; pride creates the illusion that we need nothing. People suffering from "benign" hypocrisy become aware of a contradiction in their life and run to God for help. People afflicted with "malignant" hypocrisy see the contradiction but rationalize it away, or they are so blinded by pride that they are incapable of seeing any flaws in their life. Malignant hypocrisy is like garlic; we can smell it on everyone's breath but our own.

How Dangerous Are You?

So, how dangerous are you? Are you positively dangerous? Are you placing those around you at risk of encountering the risen Lord because of the passion and the commitment with which you live your faith? Are you a tool in God's hands? Does your life shout to others that there is something better and that his name is Jesus?

Or are you more on the negatively dangerous side? Maybe your enthusiasm for your faith is less than compelling. Maybe you are aware of contradictions in your life that stand in the way of your relationship with Jesus and create a stumbling block to others. Maybe your life doesn't look all that different from the life of people who have little or no faith.

The Good News is that Jesus passionately loves you, no matter what side of "dangerous" you fall on. If you are more or less negatively dangerous, Jesus loves you enough to call you to something greater. The Kingdom of God is populated with people who were once negatively dangerous: Mary Magdalene, Matthew, Zacchaeus, and Paul. Jesus wants to change you, like these people, from the inside out. He wants to empower you. He wants to help you become a transformer of the world. He wants to make you rich in the Kingdom of God.

Becoming Positively Dangerous

The first step in becoming positively dangerous is to be honest with yourself and with God. Examine your life. Ask the Holy Spirit to help you see your life from God's perspective and to show you the choices you're making that keep you from fully loving God and from experiencing God's love for you. You can hear the Holy Spirit in prayer and through your conscience, which you form by reading the Scriptures and understanding what the Church teaches about them. The Holy Spirit also speaks to you through people in your life, such as your parents, pastors, and others who love God and want what is best for you. The Holy Spirit will never contradict what is written in the Scriptures.

The Holy Spirit will never say, "You are a bad person." Instead, the Holy Spirit points out specific areas of your life that you need to change. The voice of the Holy Spirit is gentle and kind, not harsh and demanding. The Holy Spirit leaves you with hope and encouragement. If you are feeling discouraged and hopeless, it is not the Holy Spirit who is speaking.

If the Holy Spirit convicts you of any sin in your life that stands in the way of your being positively dangerous, turn away from that sin and toward God's will. Make a 180-degree turn. Be repentant, confess your sin, and seek God's forgiveness and grace. Remember, you have been given a wonderful gift in the sacrament of Reconciliation (also called the sacrament of Penance). Although you don't need to wait for the sacrament of Reconciliation to pray to God and to ask for forgiveness, you will experience God's grace in a special way through celebrating this sacrament (see James 5:16).

Finally, pray to Jesus to give you the strength, wisdom, and grace to be positively dangerous for the Kingdom.

Questions for Reflection and Discussion

1. What does the word *dangerous* mean to you? In what ways do you find danger unattractive? In what ways are you attracted to danger?

2. How would you define the term *positively dangerous?*

3. Everyone who calls himself or herself Catholic or Christian is already dangerous. The real question is, "Are we positively dangerous or negatively dangerous?" How would you answer this question about your own life?

4. Apathetic faith is described as lifeless and indifferent. Why is apathetic faith so negatively dangerous to others?

5. On a scale from one to ten (one is bland, cottage-cheese faith, and ten is spicy, jalapeÖo faith), rate your current faith experience. Please explain why you chose that number on the scale.

6. It is easy to identify hypocrisy in others but more difficult to see it in yourself. Are you aware of any areas in your life where you say one thing but do another? What are they?

7. Have you ever been affected by the hypocrisy of others? If so, how? Why is hypocrisy so dangerous?

8. What is the first step to becoming positively dangerous on God's behalf?

Chapter 2 **Positively Dangerous**

Telemachus was a monk who lived a simple and quiet life in Asia Minor in about A.D. 400. While praying in his monastery one day, he felt God calling him to pack his bags and head for Rome. The puzzled Telemachus could not understand why God would want him to leave the peace of his monastery for the bustling metropolis of the world's most important city. Terrified, but sure of God's call, Telemachus packed a satchel with all his possessions, swung it over his shoulder, and took leave for Rome.

Having no idea why he was going to Rome, Telemachus got caught up in a large procession of excited inhabitants as he entered the city. He arrived during the commotion of a holiday festival and a triumphant celebration for a recent battle victory over the Goths. Looking for guidance or hints to God's purposes, Telemachus followed the jubilant crowds into the Colosseum for a celebratory circus.

For over four centuries, this structure was home for some of the greatest gladiatorial contests in the Roman Empire. The savagery of these contests would make the WWF (World Wrestling Federation) seem like simple child's play. Most often, the gladiators were political prisoners or slaves who were sentenced to fight to their own or their opponent's death for the amusement of the bloodthirsty crowds. The Roman spectators were exhilarated by the sight of blood and guts and by the death of animals and human beings. Even though priests and bishops spoke out against the cruelty of these barbaric practices, the populace largely ignored their words.

[handwritten note: people today don't listen to clergy when they speak out.]

Telemachus sat in the towering stands with eighty thousand shrieking spectators. He heard the roar of the lions bellowing deep within the bowels of the colossal structure. He listened to the racket of gladiatorial contestants preparing for deadly combat. He realized the crowd only got more excited by the clamor of each ensuing bloodbath. Telemachus trembled as the contestants steadfastly marched onto the floor of the arena and stopped before the emperor, crying out, "We, who are about to die, salute thee."

As the gladiators began to clash viciously with one another, Telemachus stormed down the steps toward the floor of the amphitheater. He was astounded by the brutality of the so-called sport and by the crowd's callous disregard for human life in the name of amusement. He knew he couldn't simply leave or, even worse, idly watch the savagery. He had to do something lasting, and so he leaped to the sand floor and meekly implored the crowds, "In the name of Christ, stop!" Of course, the mob hardly noticed the little monk. He darted back and forth among the battling contestants, shouting, "In the name of Christ, stop!" When the spectators finally took notice of him, they thought he must be some type of clown offering comic relief. They roared with laughter and howled in amusement.

Soon their patience wore thin, as tiny Telemachus, standing among the muscular, warring gladiators, became a major nuisance. Striking with his cold metal shield, one of the gladiators sent Telemachus spinning across the dusty floor. Telemachus got right back up and pleaded with them to stop, in the name of Christ, their circus of violence. The spectators now saw Telemachus as a threat to their entertainment and taunted him with venomous rage. The crowd hissed, booed, and screamed while pelting Telemachus with rocks and any other projectiles they could get their hands on.

Telemachus would not yield. In his attempt to part the warriors, he distracted one of the gladiators to the point that the combatant narrowly escaped a blow from his opponent. The crowd furiously screamed, "Run him through!" With a bright flash of his sword, the distracted gladiator cut through the chest and stomach of Telemachus, who collapsed in a heap to the ground. The sand turned crimson with blood. With one last gasp of strength, Telemachus pleaded, "In the name of Christ, stop!" He died on the floor of the Colosseum.

As the spectators regained their senses, they realized the horror of what had just happened. The people became silent and quickly filed out of the amphitheater, with the words "In the name of Christ, stop!" echoing in their ears. History tells us that this crowd witnessed the last gladiatorial battle in the Roman Empire.

(Adapted from Jim Burns, *Radically Committed,* p. 45)

Telemachus was so *positively dangerous* that his witness to Christ changed the views and savage practices of an entire empire.

The Need for a Bold Example Today

We live in a time when the surrounding culture is in desperate need of positively dangerous people like Telemachus. As believers in Jesus, we must become bold witnesses to his love and brave examples of his values to a spiritually starving world. The days of simply keeping our head above the raging waves of temptation are over. We cannot just be "survivors for Jesus," treading the sea of life only in hope of not drowning. We cannot be "secret agents" for Christ, working only under-cover for the Kingdom because we are not courageous enough to be counted (see Mark 8:38).

We are called, destined, and expected to be so much more. Christ calls us to be "more than conquerors" (Romans 8:37). We are called and empowered (see Acts 1:8) to impact our world positively for the Kingdom of God. Because God's plan for us is to populate heaven, our destiny is nothing less than extraordinary.

When Jesus describes his Church (which includes you and me), he says, "The gates of Hades will not prevail against it" (Matthew 16:18). Gates are not offensive weapons. Warriors do not advance on the enemy by swinging the gates. Gates are a defensive measure to hold back the enemy from advancing into a city. But we, the Church, are the conquerors breaking through the defenses of the Evil One. Empowered by the Holy Spirit, we are called to storm the gates of hell and to take territory previously held by the Evil One.

God Uses the Most Unlikely People

You may be thinking: "But I am weak. I am not the stuff of heroes. I am so average." Or you may think, "I am not even average!" Be assured that you won't be the first "nobody" God has used to change the world. History is replete with the ordinary people God uses to accomplish extraordinary feats. For example, Sarah laughs when one of Abraham's visitors prophesies that she will bear her son Isaac, for she is at a biologically impossible age to do so (see Genesis 18:9–15). Moses objects to God's call on the grounds that he suffers from a speech impediment (see Exodus 4:10–12). The widow Judith devises a plan to save her people and the Temple from the Assyrian army; she and her maid deceive the Assyrian general and win victory for the Israelites—a dangerous feat that Judith would never have dreamed of doing apart from God's call and power (see Judith 13:4–10). Jeremiah protests that he is merely an incapable child (see Jeremiah 1:4–8). The Lord instructs the prophet Samuel to go to the house of Jesse to anoint one of Jesse's sons to be King of Israel. Because Jesse doesn't consider his youngest son, David, as a candidate for anointing, he never even introduces Samuel to him (see 1 Samuel 16:1–13). Because Peter considers himself too sinful to hang out with Jesus, he pleads with Christ to leave him, even though Jesus has chosen him to be the head of the disciples (see Luke 5:1–11).

We all are worthy. God doesn't see our imperfect qualities.

God Wants to Use Us

God's use of people like Sarah, Moses, Judith, Jeremiah, David, and Peter should encourage the rest of us. Our overpowering feelings of inadequacy can paralyze us. The truth, however, is that God passionately wants to use each of us to change the world. God destines us to fulfill an exciting purpose; God has plans for our life (see Jeremiah 29:11). But the fact that God has plans and purposes for our life doesn't mean that we automatically understand them.

The story of a family of prairie chickens that lived on a plain illustrates this point. When an eagle's egg was somehow abandoned near their grass nest, the mother prairie chicken included the egg as one of her own. Once hatched, the eagle looked a little different than his prairie chicken siblings, but his family accepted him all the same.

Prairie chickens are rather lowly birds; they'll eat garbage, and they can't even fly. An eagle, on the other hand, is the most majestic of birds. It can soar to great heights, flying with grace and dignity that surpass all other birds. Now, this eagle who thought he was a prairie chicken grew up like a prairie chicken. He walked, squawked, and acted like the rest of his family.

One day, another eagle soared above this family of prairie chickens. They looked up and watched in awe the aerial feats of this majestic creature. The eagle who thought he was a prairie chicken turned to his siblings and squawked in astonishment, "Wow, look at that!" His prairie chicken brothers turned toward him and smugly remarked, "That's an eagle, the greatest of birds. You're just one of us—a lowly prairie chicken."

Sadly, that eagle died believing he was only a prairie chicken. He never thought of lifting his wings and taking flight into the domain for which he was created. The thought never occurred to him that he was destined to join his fellow eagles in the heights of the great blue sky.

You are born an eagle. You are destined to soar to the heights of God's purpose for your own life. God has created you with a plan in mind.

Being used by God has more to do with your *availability* than with your *ability.* The only person whom God cannot use is an unwilling one. We might even say that God is more able to use people who do not trust in their own abilities.

Supernatural impact requires supernatural power, which we do not possess on our own. The Holy Spirit is to a Christian what electricity is to an electrical plug: the source of strength and power. We should not approach God with an attitude of "I will do great things *for* God." The only true recipe for success in God's Kingdom begins with realizing our own inadequacies. Our attitude should be "God can do great things *through* me."

Instead of being disabled by feelings of inferiority, be enabled by the Holy Spirit's power to change this world through you.

What Positively Dangerous Is Not

Before identifying the distinguishing characteristics of danger-ous faith, I need to establish what the positively dangerous person is *not*. Positively dangerous faith is not about magnetic personalities, brilliant intelligence, or "drop-dead" attractive-ness. Positively dangerous people come in all sizes, shapes, colors, personalities, social groups, ethnic backgrounds, economic situations, and intelligence levels. Dangerous faith is not about appearance or flashiness. The positively danger-ous person doesn't shout slogans, wear clever T-shirts, and follow the latest religious fads. Dangerous faith doesn't drown out others' opinions by raising the decibels of our own. Posi-tively dangerous faith is more depth than "hype." It goes beyond being extroverted and outspoken about our faith; instead, it's an outward expression of what's inside. We can be positively dangerous whether we are socially outgoing or quietly reserved.

Positively Dangerous is a book about developing a depth of faith that gives credibility to your life by living from the inside out. You are embarking on the greatest adventure life can offer. This adventure with God involves danger and risk, and it has a cost—nothing less than your life. Anything that comes easily or costs little has no value; however, choosing to be a positively dangerous person has eternal value—for you and those you influence.

The Characteristics of a Positively Dangerous Person

What does a positively dangerous person look like? How would we recognize such a person? What are the characteris-tics of a dangerous person of faith?

Loving God

The first characteristic of a positively dangerous person of faith is his or her love for God. The single most important commandment in the Kingdom of God is to love the Lord with all our heart, soul, mind, and strength (see Mark 12:29– 30). Making our love for God our highest priority in life is the key to living justly and to having a positive impact on others.

A great orator, gifted and skilled in his craft beyond all his contemporaries, once traveled abroad to appear before sold-out audiences. His speaking ability held the most difficult crowd spellbound.

While addressing a capacity crowd, he began to recite from memory the twenty-third Psalm. "The LORD is my shepherd, I shall not want," he eloquently began. "He makes me lie down in green pastures; he leads me beside still waters; he restores my soul," he continued to articulate with perfect intonation and tempo. After the orator finished the Psalm with the grace and poise of a true master, the audience erupted in a thunderous standing ovation. The orator proudly basked in their deafening adulation.

While the applause roared, a young man in blue jeans and a sweatshirt began to make his way down the aisle toward the stage. He carried an old, worn-out Bible in his hands. He slowly climbed the stairs to the stage and approached the now curious orator. "You are so gifted!" he enthusiastically began. "The twenty-third Psalm is my favorite, and you recited it like no one I've ever heard. I was wondering, sir, if I could read it again. I am sorry that I don't have it memorized like you, but I think people would appreciate hearing it again, as you can see how positively they are responding."

"They are responding to my abilities as a world-class communicator, not to the Psalm. Go ahead and read it," he said arrogantly, hoping to prove his point by humiliating this naive kid. The orator hushed the crowd and allowed the youngster to walk to the podium.

The young man nervously fumbled through his Bible until he found the twenty-third Psalm. He cleared his throat and read: "The LORD is my shepherd, I shall not want. He makes me lie down in green pastures; he leads me beside still waters; he restores my soul." The young man's voice quivered as he made his way through the passage. The orator stood smirking, his hands folded, waiting for his opponent to be embarrassed by even attempting to recite the twenty-third Psalm at the same podium.

As the young man finished the third verse, a strange thing happened, beginning at the front left side of the auditorium. People started to weep. The emotional wave moved to the center, then to the right, and eventually overtook the entire crowd. People's hearts were touched deeply as they understood the reality of what the young man was reciting. By the time he had finished, there was not a dry eye in the place—except for those of the orator, who stood openmouthed and astonished.

The orator then motioned the young man to come over to him. He said, "Young man, in all the years I've been speaking in public, I have never received a response like that. No one has ever been so deeply touched by my words as they have been by yours today."

The young man turned to the orator, looked him in the eye, and replied, "The difference, sir, is that you know the Psalm, but I know the Shepherd."

As the story of the orator and the young man illustrates, nothing about us is absolutely dangerous if we fail to nurture our relationship with God. People who ignore their need to walk in an intimate relationship with Jesus will always be in danger, like the great orator, of being just a ministry performer. Ministry can be a scripted set of lifeless lines and Spirit-absent activities if not deeply rooted in a living spirituality. Above everything else in life, we must value our commitment to know and to love Jesus, the Shepherd, as the young man did. This fundamental first step on the road to becoming positively dangerous has absolutely no substitute.

Loving Others

The second characteristic of a positively dangerous person of faith corresponds to the second commandment of the Kingdom of God: to love others "as you love yourself" (Mark 12:31). The greatest power on earth is love. The legacy of September 11, 2001 is not the evil and destruction caused by the hatred of the al-Qaeda terrorists. Instead, it is the selfless love of the New York City police and firefighters, the Pentagon rescue workers, the passengers who foiled the plot of the terrorists on the flight that crashed in Pennsylvania, and the many who heroically sacrificed life that day for the benefit of others. Love is not only the most powerful but also the most beautiful force on this earth. Love is the most attractive, compelling, and beckoning of forces.

Propped up against a shrub in the front yard, one of many signs read, "We love you, Tyler, everyone's best friend." An entire city grieved the loss of one of the most outstanding young men in the community. Tyler Caruso, who lost his life to heart failure at the tender age of seventeen, certainly accomplished a lot in his short span of years. He was president of the student council, peer leadership advisor, program director of Hope (a drug and alcohol abuse awareness group), starting varsity middle linebacker on the football team, jazz band saxophonist, academically ranked student in the top five percent of his class, and so on. During Tyler's funeral the pastor commented that Tyler's accomplishments sounded more like those of an entire graduating class than of an individual student.

Yet, what stood out most to everyone who knew Tyler was his big heart. Friends, parents, younger siblings of friends, acquaintances, and students with special needs told story after story about how Tyler found a practical way of making them feel special, important, and loved—whether it was the unique nickname he coined for a friend's younger sibling or the rose he brought to a friend's mother whose son was absent on Mother's Day. Tyler's example was so positively dangerous that a coach from his high school suggested that the community adopt the slogan, "Be like Tyler." Tyler's example of love became an infectious standard for an entire community.

Like Tyler, people who are positively dangerous love others. As a matter of fact, Jesus expects you to build a reputation based on your love. He says that the world will know that you are his disciple "if you have love for one another" (John 13:35). Your love for others is your language to the world.

Being Authentic

The third characteristic of a positively dangerous person is authenticity. Authenticity attracts others. To be authentic is to be real, sincere, and genuine, and to be honest with others about who we are. Sincerity, like love, always draws others into our life.

I have to confess that as a father, I take special interest in watching the children of other families bicker with one another. I feel a mutual bond with their parents, who share my experience of having an imperfect family! Furthermore, I do not want to sit in the chair of a dentist who has never had a single cavity. I prefer going to a dentist who has his share of tooth decay and struggles with the daily discipline of flossing! I don't like having cavities or watching siblings fight with one another; I just relate better with real people who, like me, struggle with inconsistency and imperfection. I find it hard to relate to or connect with a perfect person.

A "holier than thou" attitude has just the opposite effect from authenticity—it repels others. I don't like being around people who wear facades, pretending to be something they are not. Any good relationship is built upon honesty. Intimacy is impossible without honesty and authenticity. Sometimes people are tempted to give the impression that they are greater and more important than they are. The following story illustrates this well.

During the Gulf War, a newly promoted colonel moved into a recently built, makeshift office. He had just arrived and was getting things organized when, out of the corner of his eye, he saw a private coming his way carrying a toolbox.

Wanting to seem important, the colonel quickly spun around and picked up his phone. "Yes, General Schwarzkopf, yes, yes, of course; I think that's an excellent plan," he said. "You've got my support on it. Thanks for checking with me. Let's touch base again soon, Norm. Good-bye." He briskly hung up and turned around.

"What can I do for you?" he asked the private. "Ah, I'm just here to hook up your phone," came the rather sheepish reply.

(Adapted from Bill Hybels and Mark Mittelberg,
Becoming a Contagious Christian, p. 57)

The positively dangerous person is real. Sincerity, genuineness, and authenticity build bridges to connect people.

Living with Integrity

We cannot be positively dangerous without possessing integrity, which is consistency. Integrity, the fourth characteristic of the positively dangerous person, means matching our inward beliefs with our outward actions, or "walking our talk." The most effective sermon we will ever preach is our life.

An unemployed young man was applying for a new position. As he filled out the application, he came across a question asking whether he had ever been arrested for a crime. Without giving the matter much thought, he wrote "no." Below this question was a second, related to the first: "Please explain why."

Not realizing this was a follow-up question only for those who had answered "yes" to the first question, the young man naively wrote, "Well, I guess I never got caught." In spite of his ruthless honesty, he was not hired.

Integrity means never having to worry about getting caught. Because you have nothing to hide, you have no need to cover up anything. What you see is what you get.

(Adapted from Frank Mercadante,
Growing Teen Disciples, pp. 32–33)

The culture around us is always trying to sell something. Most of us have been burned one time or another by a too-good-to-be-true deal that turned out to be, well, too good to be true. The result is a skeptical public. To think those around us will be interested in our faith simply because we've passionately declared, "It is the best thing that's ever happened to me," is naive. They remember all too well when people fell hook, line, and sinker for the Psychic Network Hotline. We may retort: "But this is different! This is the real thing!" They scoff, saying, "You thought that too about . . ."

People around us need evidence that our faith in Christ isn't just one more passing fad. They need to see in life a concrete illustration of the truths we believe.

Shortly after my conversion, I began to share my experience of Jesus with my friends. Most responses ranged from a polite "That's nice" to a blunt "You're a freak!" Although my immediate impact was minimal, my friends were watching me with interest. Over time they saw me resist the temptations that used to be an everyday part of my life. They started to see changes in my character, attitudes, and actions.

The change in me even began to unnerve some of my friends. I was at a party where everyone in the room was drinking except me. As people shuffled to another room in the house, I was left sitting across a table from Tim. He stared at me for a moment in silence. Suddenly he slammed down his beer can on the table and shouted, "Okay, so I am a fake!" Months earlier, the thought wouldn't have occurred to Tim that he is a fake. He was just like me and everyone else in the room. Only through the consistent witness of a transformed life could he see the possibility of something different.

When your friends see you saying no to the things that formerly enslaved you and saying yes to the things that free you, their curiosity in what you now have is aroused. Only then can you be positively dangerous.

Shortly afterward Tim and I prayed together for Jesus to enter his life.

Living on Call

Many people have jobs that require them to be "on call." For example, my friend Leo, a local firefighter and rescue diver, has left numerous gatherings to help out in situations of need. His department depends on him to carry his radio for instant communication. When Leo is on call, he is careful to be prepared and alert. To avoid inhibiting his ability to respond properly to a given emergency, he never drinks alcohol.

A positively dangerous person lives "on call" with the Holy Spirit—in other words, alert to the Holy Spirit's prompting, "making the most of the time" (Colossians 4:5).

If your faith life is as exciting as a Sunday-afternoon snooze at your Uncle Melvin's, you're probably not living on call with the Spirit! Nothing is more exciting than the adventure of being led by the Holy Spirit. Early in my faith life, I found that if I were open to the Spirit's direction, God would place me in situations where I could be of service to others and to Christ's Kingdom.

After spending most of our high school career at parties on Friday nights, a friend and I decided to try something different. We began in my car with a simple prayer that went something like this: "Lord, we give you this night. Let us be at your service. We ask you to guide us to people in need of your love. Help us to follow your prompting and do your will. Direct every turn we make, and help us end up where you want us to go, saying and doing what you want us to do."

We never had an evening when that prayer failed to be answered. Oh, there were times we didn't care for our assignment or really understand God's choice, but somehow we found our way to situations where we were able to share the Good News with others or be a source of Good News to those who needed a helping hand. Because we began to recognize the nudging of the Spirit and felt like we were interacting with the God of the universe, our faith became living, active, and real. We were experiencing adventures similar to those described by Luke in the Book of Acts.

To this day I am amazed at the opportunities God still places before me. I often find myself in "chance" encounters with people who have been resisting the call of God. In most cases they have faithful family members or friends interceding for their conversion or renewal.

The fact is that the Holy Spirit wants to use you to change your world. Moments before his Ascension, Jesus says, "But you will receive power when the Holy Spirit has come upon you; and you will be my witnesses in Jerusalem, in all Judea and Samaria, and to the ends of the earth" (Acts 1:8).

The term translated "power" in the above verse is from the Greek word *dunamis,* from which we get the word *dynamite.* In other words, you are given powerful, explosive capability. The word literally means "I am able; I am capable," which is exactly what the Holy Spirit does in the life of those who seek to be "on call." Remember that it is the Holy Spirit who transforms the Apostles from cowardly to courageous, from fearful to fearless, from confused to confident. The Holy Spirit makes them—and will make you—positively dangerous.

1. What stands out to you most in the story about Telemachus?

2. Do you agree that you live in a time when the surrounding culture is in desperate need of positively dangerous people like Telemachus? Please explain why or why not.

3. God passionately wants to use you to change the world. What is one thing you believe God may want you to do at this time in your life? How do you feel about trying to do it?

4. Being used by God has more to do with availability than ability. Do you agree or disagree? Please explain.

5. What does it mean to live "from the inside out"?

6. If you were to make loving God your highest priority, would your life be any different than it is now? If so, how?

7. What is the difference between knowing God and knowing about God?

8. Think about the people in your life. Who are among the most authentic people you know? Why do you identify them as authentic? How do you feel around them?

9. Integrity means to match your inward beliefs with your outward actions. It is the opposite of hypocrisy. Do you consider yourself to be a person of integrity? Explain.

10. Share an experience when you were "on call" for the Holy Spirit and God used you in another person's life, or share a time when someone else seemed to be "on call" and made a difference in your life.

Chapter 3
Fruit of the Vine
for the Underaged

One evening in the former Soviet Union during the mid-1970s, a dozen Christian believers gathered at the home of one of their leaders to pray and to study the Scriptures. At that time such a gathering was illegal.

The leader shut the door after the last of the believers arrived. All bowed and began the meeting with prayer. Suddenly a loud bang at the door startled the group. Before they could respond, three secret police agents burst through the door and into the meeting room. Each was tightly gripping an automatic weapon. The leader of the police quickly surveyed the room and yelled, "What's going on in here?"

The prayer group leader caught his breath and timidly responded, "We are Christians and have gathered to pray and . . ."

"What?" screamed the leader of the secret police. "Don't you know that is an illegal activity?" Pointing his AK-47 at the door, he added, "You have three minutes to walk out that door, and when you do, know that you are publicly denying Jesus Christ as your Lord and Savior."

Immediately, three members of the group scurried out the door. The leader of the secret police raised his left arm and turned his wrist to view his watch. In the other hand, he held his rifle toward the intimidated believers.

"You have two minutes," he sternly warned. Two additional members jumped to their feet and ran out the door. The remaining members gasped and stared at one another in quiet desperation.

"You have one minute." With tears streaming from his face, another individual streaked out the door to safety.

"You have thirty seconds!" the leader barked at the group. Another panicked member bolted out the door. At this point the few remaining believers nervously joined hands and began to pray and to reassure themselves with the words of the Scriptures.

With his voice raised to a crescendo, the leader of the police shrieked, "You've got five seconds!"

"That's it!" he screamed as he rushed toward the entrance and bolted shut the only avenue of escape. Quickly turning around and with his AK-47 raised, he rushed toward the terrified believers and said, "Now that the phonies are gone, let's praise Jesus!"

(Adapted from a presentation by Larry Tomczak, Catholic Charismatic Conference, 1978)

Which Side of the Door?

If you're anything like me, you're wondering on which side of the door you would find yourself. Would you be a Christian superhero or a feeble phony? We all hope that we would have the strength and the resolve to stand firm for Jesus, even in the most difficult and demanding circumstances. Yet, danger-ous commitment—the kind that places our life and security at risk—does not come without significant cost and personal investment.

Positively dangerous faith, the kind that clearly puts us in real peril and places those around us in danger of catching it, does not emerge in our life as a result of our own strength. The Apostle Peter learns this the hard way when he denies Christ three times.

Loving God Is Our True Source of Strength

Before we can place God in God's rightful authority in our life, we must begin with respect and awe for God's majesty and power. This attitude prevents us from becoming so casual with the Creator that we reduce God to creature status. But fear is only the beginning of wisdom. The highest wisdom is to love God. Loving God with all our heart, mind, and strength makes us able to be courageous, fruitful for the Kingdom of God, and positively dangerous to those around us. As a matter of fact, our level of being positively dangerous is directly proportionate to the degree to which we love God.

The truth is that all of us know and love the Lord as much as we want to. The Lord never limits our intimacy with him (see Jeremiah 29:13). Few of us make a regular practice of seeking the Lord with all our heart. We may go through reli-gious motions and get involved in spiritual activities, but few of us want to know the Lord so intimately that we are willing to give up everything else in exchange.

Obstacles to Loving God

What stands in our way of seeking God and loving the Lord with all our heart, mind, and strength? What are some of the common barriers that threaten to block our passage to a deeper relationship with God?

Fear That God Doesn't Have Our Best Interests in Mind

While growing up, I had respect for God, but I had a difficult time trusting the Lord with my everyday life. I didn't want to end up in hell in the future, but I didn't want God running my life in the present. Deep down I thought Jesus would ruin my life if I gave him control of it. I was deceived by the "sinners have more fun" mentality. I figured I knew better than God did, but I wasn't the first person to think this way. The fear that "God doesn't have my best interests in mind" begins with Adam and Eve (see Genesis 2:16,17; 3:1; 3:2–5).

At the heart of every temptation is the notion that we cannot trust God's intentions. God is holding back the good life from us, and the only way to experience it is to take our life into our own hands. Adam and Eve quickly find out that God's intentions are in their best interests, but by then it is too late.

We too can be deceived by this lie. We can keep God at arm's length, trying to be friendly enough to avoid the extremes of hell but distant enough to elude Jesus in our life. The result is spiritual mediocrity, a bland, cottage-cheese existence. Not only will we never experience the abundant life Jesus promises here on earth (see John 10:10), but also we will live with an eternity of regret that we did not have more trust in God's goodness. The ultimate experience of life is living it with Jesus at the center. Life doesn't get any better than that.

Nearsighted Living

Another barrier that keeps us from experiencing a close relationship with God is nearsighted living. We become spiritually nearsighted when we get so caught up with the offerings and activities of this world that we reduce the role of Jesus in our life to one among many offerings of a healthy lifestyle. The problem is that Jesus never suggests that he should be one of many spokes on the wheel of our balanced life. Jesus calls us to nothing less than total commitment. Our Lord calls us to exclusive love (see Luke 14:26).

Is Jesus literally calling us to hate those closest to us? Absolutely not! Jesus is using hyperbole, or exaggeration, to make a point. Jesus is saying that our love for him should be far and above our love for anyone or anything, including ourselves. When we love Jesus above all else, we will love those around us with a love that far surpasses our own capabilities.

Too often our lack of love for God is the result of getting caught up in things that simply don't matter. Our treasures—those things that occupy our heart and motivate our decisions—can become the things of this world (see Matthew 6:19–21). We can order our life according to activities and issues that have little or no eternal value. We end up majoring on the minors and minoring on the majors.

This spiritual nearsightedness is well illustrated in the story of the ambitious college freshman who was conversing with her wise, older professor. After class the young woman outlined her life plans to her professor: "I am going to graduate *magna cum laude* and go to Harvard Law School."

The professor responded, "Then what?"

The young woman confidently replied, "I will join a prestigious New York City law firm and become a partner within five years."

The professor raised his eyebrows and asked, "Then what?"

Without skipping a beat, the freshman added, "I will run for the New York State Legislature, win, and serve three terms."

"And then?" the professor asked.

"I will run for the United States Senate, win, and serve six terms."

"Then what will you do?" the professor asked.

"I will buy a home in Florida, retire, and enjoy life," the young woman said with a sense of completion.

"What then?" the professor asked again.

Bewildered, the young woman muttered, "I guess I'll die!"

The professor paused for several seconds and asked one more time, "Then what?"

The young woman blankly stared at him.

"You fool!" the professor said. "You have so carefully mapped out your life without ever a thought about your eternity."

Jesus is speaking of spiritual nearsightedness when he says: "For those who want to save their life will lose it, and those who lose their life for my sake will find it. For what will it profit them if they gain the whole world but forfeit their life? Or what will they give in return for their life?" (Matthew 16:25–26).

The Apostle Paul warns us when he writes, "Set your minds on things that are above, not on things that are on earth" (Colossians 3:2). Furthermore, Paul puts things in perspective and gives us a clear vision of life when he states: "More than that, I regard everything as loss because of the surpassing value of knowing Christ Jesus my Lord. For his sake I have suffered the loss of all things, and I regard them as rubbish, in order that I may gain Christ" (Philippians 3:8–9). Paul is spiritually farsighted. He orders his life by his love for Jesus and by the eternal values of the Kingdom of God.

Lack of Discipline

My daughter Sarah dreams of running a marathon. I might not consider her too bright if she just shows up at the starting line on the day of the race. Instead, to be fully prepared for the physical demands of the race, she wisely is developing a regular schedule of training over these next several months. In the same way, intimacy with God will not come by sheer desire alone.

Once a very famous and incredibly skilled pianist performed a concert in a sold-out music hall. Afterward, he spent a few minutes talking with some audience members. One woman walked up to him and enthusiastically exclaimed, "I would do anything to be able to play the piano like you." The man paused for a moment and replied, "No, you wouldn't."

The world-renowned pianist knew that if she were willing to do "anything" to play like he does, she too would share his skills. He was well aware of the endless hours he had invested over the years to develop his present abilities. It's easy to say, "I'll do anything to have those skills," but an entirely different matter to do those things. That's precisely why excelling in any activity has such value in our eyes. The cost of excelling gives it value. The spiritual life is no different.

To grow in our love and knowledge of the Lord will require an investment of time on our part. It is imperative to schedule consistent time in our life to be in the Lord's presence. There is no substitute for integrating regular practices into our life that place us in a position to be transformed. (I will examine these practices in greater detail in chapter 4.)

We need to do everything we can to clear the path of any barriers that stand in the way of building a deep relationship with Jesus. We might believe the misconception that God doesn't have our best interests in mind. Perhaps we are too caught up in worldly matters to care about God's Kingdom, or maybe we lack the discipline to make time for God. In each case we need to ask God for the grace to make our relationship with Jesus the highest priority in our life.

Life as It Is Meant to Be

Have you ever had a conversation with someone who is close to death and knows it? Such a person doesn't waste words on idle chatter like, "What's the weather out there?" Instead, a dying person measures words by the reality of the limited time available and tends to say what is most important.

At the Last Supper, knowing that he is a dying man with only a few hours to finish preparing the disciples for their mission of bringing the Gospel to the ends of the earth, Jesus reveals the teaching of the vine and branches (see John 15:1–8).

Jesus makes some things very clear to his disciples. First, he puts an end to the idea that anyone is going to do great things *for* God (see John 15:4). If we are going to do anything of lasting value (fruit), it will be the result *only* of being relationally connected to Jesus. God is going to do things *through* us. Our harvest of fruit is directly proportionate to our degree of abiding with Jesus, who is the vine.

We cannot be positively dangerous without a vital, living, and ongoing relational connection to Jesus. Know Jesus, know abundant fruit; no Jesus, no fruit. If we want to make a difference in eternity, we will have to invest time in learning how to walk intimately with Jesus.

A Relationship Beyond Just Bearing Fruit

Although we are meant to bear fruit as disciples of Christ (see John 15:8), our relationship with Jesus is not simply for that purpose. Consider a person who is our friend only because the friendship will boost his or her popularity and gain him or her entry into a more prestigious peer group. How demeaning that would be to us as the friend! What kind of friendship would that be? Instead, friendship should be for the sake of the relationship, not for what we can gain from it.

In the same manner, spiritual fruit is a natural result of spiritual intimacy and union with Jesus. We shouldn't establish a business relationship with Jesus only to be spiritually successful. We can easily become professionals at serving God and amateurs at being the Lord's friend. Jesus is a person, first and foremost, who wants to be in a loving relationship with us. Jesus wants us to know and to experience his love for us.

This love—this crazy kind of love—drives Jesus to the cross to suffer and die an excruciating death on our behalf (see Romans 5:7–8). This is the love that Jesus wants us to experience by relationally abiding in him. Our first call is not to be fruitful or to make a difference. Our first call is to Jesus—to love him and to experience his love for us (see Revelation 2:1–7). Jesus is not asking us to do more *for* him. He is asking us to be more *with* him. Jesus' desire is to be our closest, most intimate companion. The fruit in our life and the impact we make are a natural result of our loving Jesus. As Saint Augustine so wisely says, "Love God, and do as you please" (*Sermons on the First Epistle of John,* 7:8).

Scheduling Time in Our Life

We cannot fulfill our true destiny without making our relationship with Jesus our first priority. Yet, developing an intimate relationship with Jesus will not come without exertion; it will require effort on our part. First, we must raise our relationship with Jesus to be the highest priority and the greatest pursuit in our life. Friendships do not flourish unless friends spend time together. We must schedule Jesus into his rightful place in our life. We should set aside *focused* time each day to be with Jesus.

Jesus is the ultimate model for setting aside time to be recharged in prayer. When he walks among us on the earth, even though he is both human and the Son of God, he finds it necessary to be alone in prayer with God. Jesus is in high demand and extremely busy, yet he is never too busy to neglect his relationship with the Father (see Mark 1:35). The fact is that if we are too busy to pray, we are too busy.

Choosing a Time

The first practical step in establishing a meaningful quiet time is finding the right period of day to schedule it. Often our level of spiritual success has more to do with practical things than with issues of the heart. For example, we may want to nurture a relationship with Jesus, but because we schedule our focused prayer time just before bed, we end up "sleeping before God" instead of "seeking God." We must consider some practical issues when choosing our prayer time.

On page 50 you will find a table that represents a weekly schedule. Fill in the details of your typical week, including all your activities, commitments, and meetings for each day. Next ask yourself: "When am I most alert and least distracted? When am I focused enough to have meaningful interaction with God?" To reflect God's priority in your life, it is important to give God the best of your available options. The Jews in the Old Testament refer to this as the "first fruits." They consider it insulting, even sacrilegious, to give God anything less than the best of their crops or herds. Consider a "best friend" who is only willing to give your relationship a few hectic, leftover minutes during the chaos between class periods. Your friendship would suffer and possibly die over time.

After reviewing your schedule and considering those times of the day when you are most alert and able to concentrate, write "prayer time" in a time slot that works best for you. Find the best *available* option. If possible, schedule your prayer time during the same period each day, which will become a routine part of your life in no time.

Time Duration

The next question you need to answer is, "How much should I set aside for my quiet time?" Be cautious not to begin by being overly zealous with spiritual ambition. Novice skiers don't make their first run on the expert course in Vale. They would do best to take to the bunny slope. In the same way, choose an amount of time that is realistic for you. It is always smarter to start small and steadily progress than to begin big and fall hard. Small successes will build momentum, fueling you with the encouragement you need to tackle greater mountains. If you are a novice in prayer, consider beginning with a ten- to fifteen-minute slot. As you progress, that time may grow into an hour or more.

Choosing a Place

Once you have decided on a time, the next important step is to choose the right place. Selecting a place that is as loud and chaotic as a classroom of hyperactive preschoolers would prove to be too much for the most selective of hearing. Find a location where you can be alone and undisturbed. Move away from the distractions of people, televisions, stereos, and telephones.

Additionally, your prayer spot must be convenient. If it requires a forty-five minute commute to get there, it's impractical. You may find yourself with a less than ideal situation as a result of sharing a room with a sibling or being in a cramped home. Nevertheless, find your best available option. Remember that God understands your situation and honors your honest efforts.

Finally, make your prayer space spiritually inviting by creating an environment that reminds you of God's presence. Praying near a computer, school assignments, or your Sony PlayStation may prove to be too tempting for even the most iron-willed of saints. Instead, assemble a place of prayer for yourself. Creating a favorable environment may include the placement of candles, religious pictures, a cross, a crucifix, or other spiritually significant items.

Some Final Thoughts

The first and most important characteristic of being positively dangerous is to love God with all our heart, mind, and strength. To do so we must address the obstacles that stand in the way of making our relationship with Jesus our highest priority. As is true with all relationships, we need to devote time to develop our relationship with Christ. Taking the practical step to schedule time alone with God and to find the right location for prayer is an essential first step. Filling that time with meaningful interaction with God will make the investment pay dividends. Chapter 4 will focus on this topic.

Daily Schedule

The table includes the seven days of the week, divided into fifteen- to thirty-minute blocks, beginning at your earliest hour and ending late in the evening, as in the following format:

Time	Sunday	Monday	Tuesday	Wednesday	Thursday	Friday	Saturday
5:00 a.m.							
5:15 a.m.							
5:30 a.m.							
5:45 a.m.							
6:00 a.m.							
. . . .							

Questions for Reflection and Discussion

1. In the story about Christians in the former Soviet Union, what is the difference between the people who stayed (thinking they were going to be shot) and those who bolted from the room?

2. Your level of being positively dangerous is directly proportionate to the degree to which you love God. Do you agree or disagree? Why?

3. Which of the three obstacles that stand in your way of loving God is the most difficult for you: fear that God doesn't have your best interests in mind? nearsighted living? lack of discipline?

4. What is one practical step you can take to overcome the obstacle you identified?

5. You cannot be positively dangerous without a vital, living, and ongoing relational connection to Jesus. On a scale from one to ten (one is the most distant, and ten is your closest, most intimate companion), how would you rate the closeness of your relationship with Jesus at this time?

6. What is one thing you can do to take a step closer to Jesus?

7. In what ways have you experienced Jesus' personal love for you?

8. Because building a friendship with Jesus requires intentional effort and setting aside a focused time each day, what are you currently doing or what do you need to do to have this special time with Jesus?

9. What is the best time and where is the best location for your daily prayer? What steps can you take to ensure that this time and place are set aside for prayer?

Chapter 4
Getting Disciplined

On February 21, 2002, in Salt Lake City, Utah, sixteen-year-old Sarah Hughes experienced the thrill of victory as she donned the Olympic gold medal for ladies' figure skating. A surprised audience shared her dream come true after watching her history-making performance. Although Sarah's figure-skating skills were proven prior to the 2002 Winter Olympics, her capture of the gold medal after entering the free-skate in fourth place was a huge surprise to all.

Sarah's victory was a surprise, but it was no accident. She had spent years training to accomplish her sharply focused goal of being an Olympic athlete. The discipline of untold hours of practice, injuries, inevitable setbacks, and just plain hard work preceded her moment of glory. Sarah didn't just show up on the ice that February evening. She had begun as a novice at the age of three and made the commitment to develop her skills through years of intentional training and practice.

Becoming an Olympic champion like Sarah takes time, sacrifice, and discipline. So too does developing a meaningful relationship with Christ. Growing in this relationship, as in any other relationship, requires effort and spiritual discipline. Saint Paul says it this way: "Athletes exercise self-control in all things; they do it to receive a perishable wreath, but we an imperishable one" (1 Corinthians 9:25). Just as athletes perform physical exercises to become physically fit, we take on spiritual exercises to become spiritually fit. The more spiritually fit we are, the more positively dangerous we become.

The Spiritual Discipline of Solitude

Our training to become spiritually fit begins with the spiritual discipline of *solitude,* which basically means "to be alone with God." Jesus regularly practices the discipline of solitude to connect himself more closely to the Father. Mark writes, "In the morning, while it was still very dark, he got up and went out to a deserted place, and there he prayed" (Mark 1:35; see also Matthew 4:1–11; Mark 6:31; Luke 6:12). Solitude is being alone, away from people, the media, and other interactions, to be with God.

This time alone, or solitude, with God slows us down to a pace that allows us to view our life and our very self from God's viewpoint. So often our life is filled with haste, hurry, and distraction. Just as we can't accurately see the contents of a storefront display while driving by at the speed limit, we can't get a good view of our life if we're always in high gear. Without solitude we find ourselves following the frenzied flow of traffic with no real direction. Solitude is the needed rest stop that gives us time to examine the direction we are taking so that we can journey toward the priorities of God's Kingdom rather than toward the values and priorities of the world around us.

Setting aside a special time each day to practice solitude is an excellent way to begin. As we advance in the practice of solitude, we may consider extending our time alone with God from five minutes to fifteen, to thirty, and eventually to an hour. We may consider devoting an extended period of time to solitude, such as two to three hours in an afternoon, or even a one-day retreat.

Solitude and Other Spiritual Exercises

You've decided to show up for spiritual training by setting aside time for solitude, so what's next? Solitude is almost always practiced with other spiritual exercises, such as silence, prayer, study, and meditation. You can use your time of solitude to study or meditate upon the Scriptures, to pray, or to be silent in God's presence.

The Spiritual Discipline of Silence

Let's learn more about what to do during our prayer time from one of the most wonderful spiritual coaches in the history of the Catholic Church. Mother Teresa lived a life of poverty, caring for the poorest of the poor in Calcutta, India. She won the Nobel Peace Prize in 1979, and her life remains an inspiration to the entire world. Mother Teresa was without question a positively dangerous woman of faith; through her simple obedience to God's call in her life, she influenced millions to greater love of God and others.

Faced with the urgent needs of dying, neglected, and destitute people, Mother Teresa knew that she could serve others only by remaining close to Christ. She once remarked, "I'm only a little wire—God is the power" (*Mother Teresa: A Simple Path,* p. xi). She received power from God by making solitude a priority in her life, and she required the same of all the Sisters of Charity and Brothers of the Word who served alongside her.

Mother Teresa said: "I always begin my prayer in silence, for it is in the silence of the heart that God speaks. God is the friend of silence—we need to listen to God because it's not what we say but what He says to us and through us that matters" (*Mother Teresa: A Simple Path,* p. 7).

The two spiritual disciplines of solitude and silence work hand in hand to help create a depth where truly positive danger resides. Silence means abstaining from outer words, noise, and music to distinguish the inner voice of God. Silence focuses on listening to the voice of God. Through the discipline of silence, we begin to recognize God's voice in our life.

We learn to distinguish the voice of God in the same way sheep learn to recognize the voice of their shepherd. A visitor to the Middle East once described an experience of three shepherds and their flocks, all meeting at a small lake. He became concerned as the flocks intermingled while drinking at the water's edge. To his surprise, the shepherds engaged in friendly conversation with one another, apparently unconcerned that their sheep were blending into one indistinguishable flock.

After several minutes the shepherds started afoot, but in opposite directions. Each sang while walking. Like a marching-band formation that begins in chaos only to emerge in recognizable order and design, the three flocks began forming distinguishable lines of bleating sheep that followed the song of their shepherd. Not a lamb wavered in confusion. They all clearly recognized the voice of their shepherd and followed his lead.

(Adapted from Rick Joyner, *A Prophetic Vision for the 21st Century,* p. 74)

The sheep learned to recognize the voice of their shepherd because they had spent a lot of time in their shepherd's presence. The same is true in the Christian life. We learn to distinguish the voice of the Lord while spending time in the silent presence of God.

However, we all begin as lambs in distinguishing God's voice. A lamb learning to recognize the voice of its shepherd relies on the older sheep in the flock. Lambs follow the lead and direction of the older, more experienced sheep. Likewise, young believers need to rely on the wisdom and spiritual maturity of more experienced community members, spiritual mentors, and Church authorities. The Lord speaks through the words and life of other faithful believers.

The Spiritual Discipline of Reading the Scriptures

In 1847 an ailing woman was preparing her will. Prior to her death, this woman, who loved and treasured the Scriptures, filled her family Bible with cash amounting to about $5,000, a large sum of money in those days. Along with her Bible, she left a small sum of money to her nephew.

The woman's will read, "To my beloved nephew, Steven Marsh, I will and bequeath my family Bible and all it contains, with the residue of my estate after my funeral expenses and just and lawful debts are paid." The estate (apart from the $5,000 in her Bible) amounted to a few hundred dollars. Steven, then a young man, not giving a second thought to the Bible and "all it contains," soon spent the few hundred dollars. He put the soon-to-be-forgotten leather-bound Bible with its brass clasps on the shelf and never opened it once.

For thirty-five years Steven lived in poverty, receiving only a small government pension. Toward the end of his life, he decided to move and live with his son. While he was packing his trunk, the forgotten cash fell from the tattered Bible, and he gathered and counted it. Waves of regret flooded his heart when he realized that he had been living as a pauper for thirty-five years when he was actually a rich man. He didn't know that a much better life had been within his grasp.

Steven's misfortune can be ours as well. God has given us a costly treasure of wisdom and knowledge, of grace and love, in his Word. The Scriptures make us spiritually rich and show us how to live as sons and daughters of God. The truth in the Scriptures brings clarity, peace, and happiness to our life. Yet, like Steven, most of us don't take the time to open and appreciate the Scriptures. We live like spiritual orphans while God would lavish upon us the riches of the Kingdom. A better life awaits if only we would open the Word of God.

Reading the Scriptures is one of the main ways we learn to recognize God's voice in our life and thereby grow closer to Jesus. A steady diet of the Word of God is essential for proper spiritual nutrition. The Scriptures are full of promises, words of encouragement, directions for living, and insights into who God is. We will live an anemic Christian life, at best, without regularly studying, praying, and living out the Scriptures.

Many methods and approaches to reading, studying, and meditating upon the Scriptures are available, but the first step is to make a plan. You may begin by following the lectionary (the Church's daily readings) or by reading one of the books in the Bible, such as the Gospel of John. Start by asking the Holy Spirit to guide you and to reveal the insights you need most. Read the Scriptures slowly and reflectively while considering these questions: What does this passage tell me about God? about living? about what to do in my life today?

It is always important to subject your insights to the historical context, to the whole Bible, and to the Church's teaching. Interpreting a passage outside these protective boundaries can place you in dangerous waters. You must understand what the author is trying to express to the audience for whom he is writing. To do this you need to know something about what is going on in their community, in their culture, and in history. You can usually obtain this background from the introduction to the chapter in your Bible. *The Catholic Youth Bible* (Winona, MN: Saint Mary's Press, 2000), for example, includes introductions and commentaries along with the text. If you need further information, you can look in more specialized books, called "commentaries," which go a lot deeper.

Once you understand what the writer of the Scriptures is trying to say to the particular group (the Corinthians, the Thessalonians, the Galatians, and so on), you can apply the message to your life and time. One rule of thumb when reading the Scriptures and applying them to your life is that if you come up with something radical (like quitting school to devote yourself full-time to prayer), it is wise to talk to someone else before you carry it out. Also, the teaching of the Church is the result of thorough study of the Scriptures over many centuries. Church teaching, most easily found in *The Catechism of the Catholic Church,* is an important guide for understanding the Scriptures and applying them to your life.

The Spiritual Discipline of Prayer

Prayer—talking with, listening to, and spending quality time with the Lord—is fundamental for spiritual growth. "Prayer feeds the soul—as blood is to the body, prayer is to the soul—and it brings you closer to God" (*Mother Teresa: A Simple Path,* p. 7). Without prayer we cannot have a relationship with God. Prayer has many approaches, methods, and stages, but the bottom line is that we need to pray.

First, prayer is a relationship. It's not about gritting our teeth while reciting prayers. It's about falling in love. It's not about duty but about spending time with our most intimate companion. Prayer is about seeking, loving, longing, waiting, and being with the one we love. Much of our time with Jesus is the company and conversation of two close friends. The long-term result of this relationship is that we learn to love God, we allow God to love us, and we become equipped to be positively dangerous to those around us.

The acronym **PRAY** describes a useful process for prayer. First, we begin with **P**raise. When we take our eyes off Jesus, we slip into a spiritual slump. When we praise God, we shift our eyes from ourselves and our problems to a square focus on Jesus. This refocusing gives us a true perspective in life. Instead of beginning prayer by being overwhelmed with our own big problems, we overwhelm our problems by remembering how big our God is.

Thanksgiving and adoration are the Siamese twins of praise. In thanksgiving we honor the Lord for what God has done for us; in adoration we magnify the Lord and focus on what we love about God.

Expressing a sense of gratitude does not come naturally to most of us. In infancy we innately demand, with the tenacity of a dive-bombing mosquito, that our desires be fulfilled. We wail our want for a diaper change; we scream our way to the next meal. But being grateful is an entirely different story. With great effort and endless repetition, our parents teach us to say thank you. Expressing our thanks to God is not instinctive. We have to learn the discipline of "giving thanks to God the Father at all times and for everything in the name of our Lord Jesus Christ" (Ephesians 5:20).

Adoration focuses on the person of God: adoring, honoring, blessing, and exalting the Lord. In adoration we speak the truth about God's goodness, holiness, power, and love. We cherish God for being God.

God does not need our praise; the Lord does not ache for our affirmation. We need to adore God; our souls ache for the Lord. Adoring God is like being fitted with corrective lenses: we scan the horizon of life with true perspective. We see our life from the only accurate vantage point—under the guidance, protection, and love of an all-powerful, all-good, and all-loving God.

Among the infinite reasons to adore God, let me suggest several aspects of the Lord's essence that can lead us to praise: God's wisdom, love, holiness, power, justice, righteousness, integrity, loyalty, mercy, kindness, compassion, and faithfulness. We can express praise in many ways: saying spontaneous words from the heart, singing, dancing, changing posture, composing and saying prayers of praise, reading the Scriptures (especially the Psalms), and celebrating the Eucharist.

The second element of **PRAY** is **R**equest. A prayer of request, often called a prayer of supplication, is the act of asking God for something. Jesus wants us to present our needs to God, as when he teaches us to pray, "Give us this day our daily bread" (Matthew 6:11).

The two principle expressions of a prayer of request are *petition* and *intercession.* Petition is the act of asking on behalf of yourself. Asking God to help *you* do well on your history test is an example of a prayer of petition. The second expression of a prayer of request, intercession, is the act of asking God on behalf of *others.* Praying that your friend Amy does well on her history test is an example of an intercessory prayer.

"The more, the better" is a good principle when we need prayer in our life. We have our earthly family and friends to pray for us, and we also have our heavenly family rooting for us. Relatives who have gone before us in death and the saints who have already passed the finish line are ready and willing to pray for us. Just ask them to pray for you or for someone you're concerned about. If you've been confirmed and have taken on a saint's name, you may want to ask that saint to pray for you.

Developing a prayer list or a journal is one way of organizing our prayers of request. By keeping track of our prayer requests, we ensure that we consistently remember important needs. Additionally, we are able to adjust the list or write notes on the progress of particular needs. Finally, a record of our prayer requests can serve as a faith builder as we witness God intervening through our focused efforts. The following format can serve as a prayer list:

Date	Prayer Request / Need	Answer Date	Answer / Notes

The third element of **PRAY** is **A**udit. The accountant who carefully examines the financial dealings of a company or an individual in light of proper and lawful accounting principles is performing a financial audit. A spiritual audit is similar: examining the interactions of our life in light of the presence and the teachings of Jesus. By carefully reviewing our behavior in thought, word, action, and inaction each day, we inspect how well we are following the Lord and the commandments of God's Kingdom.

We spiritually audit our day from two perspectives. The first perspective is an examination of *consciousness.* We ask,

"How conscious was I of God's presence today?" The Lord is always present and working in our life, but did we pay attention to God throughout our day? Without examining our life through the eyes of faith, we can be blind to God's rich involvement in our day.

Jesus is often present in routine events and encounters. For example, while writing this section of the book, I noticed that the computer screen was very blurry when I looked at it through my left eye. Having put on my contacts earlier, I figured I needed to clean the left lens. When I tried to remove the lens, I realized that it had never made it onto my eye in the first place! I searched and prayed. Incredibly I found the lens, dried and hard, on my bathroom floor. After soaking for a few minutes, the lens softened and resumed its shape, and I was able to use it to see again. While prayerfully reflecting on the situation, I was reminded and comforted by God's care of my life, even in the most minute details. God was with me this morning.

Another example of examining our life in light of God's presence includes reflecting on difficult situations. Perhaps you had an encounter with an obnoxious classmate during lunch. Maybe, beyond your initial annoyance with his arrogance, there is a divine opportunity here. The Lord may be speaking to you about the deeper pain and hurt that causes a person who acts like this to assert himself with conceit. Perhaps God is calling you to respond differently in the future in light of this new understanding. The discipline of examining our consciousness trains us to see God's fingerprints on the most mundane events and encounters.

The second perspective of a spiritual audit involves making an examination of *conscience*. We ask the Holy Spirit to point out to us the areas of our life that need God's cleansing, healing, and corrective direction. We ask the loving Lord to scrutinize our life. The result of this form of examination is the self-knowledge without which we cannot progress spiritually. We learn the truth about ourselves—our strengths, weaknesses, vulnerabilities, and areas of faithfulness. Sometimes what we see is not all that attractive—jealousy, envy, hatred, dishonesty, lust, greed, pride, and the like. The good news is that we don't face our sinful tendencies alone; we face them with an all-accepting and loving God. We find our greatest friend, who knows us in our entirety yet loves us entirely. We find Jesus, who can judge and condemn us but chooses not to (see John 8:1–11). Through facing our sinful tendencies and bringing them to Christ each day and regularly in the sacrament of Reconciliation, we become intimately acquainted with God's love, grace, and forgiveness.

In human relationships we often fear revealing our vulnerabilities to others. They may not like us because of our weaknesses or use them against us. Revealing our innermost person to Jesus has the opposite effect. We walk away feeling more loved, secure, and strengthened. As we experience God's compassion toward us in spite of our failures, we learn to accept others, and we become more compassionate with their weaknesses.

In addition to making a spiritual audit during your prayer time, you should do one before you go to sleep each night. Prayerfully ask (consciousness audit) "Jesus, in what ways were you present in my life today?" and (conscience audit) "Jesus, examine my thoughts, words, and interactions. In what ways could I have better loved you and those around me?" If you are a verbal learner, you may consider answering these questions in a daily spiritual journal to help keep track of the patterns, issues, and progress of your spiritual life.

The last element in **PRAY** is **Y**ield. Initially prayer is anything but yielding to God! We are more concerned about begging, brooding, pleading, and pouting. We are like manipulative children demanding, "I want what I want when I want it!" Instead of seeking God's will, we seek to convince God of our will. We search for the right combination that unlocks the genie god who exists to fulfill our every wish.

This normal beginning to prayer, over a period of time, gives way to surrender prayer. As we become better acquainted with the absolute wisdom and goodness of God, we begin to trust the Lord with more and more of our life. Here we begin to understand one of the paradoxes of God's Kingdom: true surrender brings total victory. Countries that sign a treaty of unconditional surrender concede military defeat. They are the losers! However, when we surrender our will to Jesus, we experience true victory. We are the winners! The essence of prayer is to take us to a place of surrender. Prayer is not about bending the will of a reluctant god but about bending our reluctant will to the will of a loving and perfect God. Prayer changes us.

Consider one final piece of advice from Mother Teresa:

> Our total surrender to God means to be entirely at the disposal of the Father as Jesus and Mary were. In giving ourselves completely to God, because God has given himself to us, we are entirely at his disposal,
> — to be possessed by him so that we may possess him,
> — to take whatever he gives and to give whatever he takes with a big smile,
> — to be used by him as it pleases him without being consulted,
> — to offer him our free will, our reason, our whole life in pure faith, so that he may think his thoughts in our minds, do his work through our hands, and love with our hearts.
>
> (*Total Surrender,* pp. 35–36)

Saint Paul invites us to "run in such a way that you may win" (1 Corinthians 9:24). We can begin our training now and eventually join the ranks of the spiritual Olympians who have gone before us. As we make time for solitude and as we practice listening to God, praising God, requesting what we need from God, yielding to God, and reading the Scriptures, we will grow closer to the Lord each day and will be well on our way to becoming positively dangerous people of faith.

Questions for Reflection and Discussion

1. Is there an area of your life in which you've had to exert a lot of discipline to succeed? If so, share your experience. If not, perhaps you can share an example from someone else's life.

2. How comfortable are you with silence in your life? What are some of the challenges? What are some of the benefits?

3. What role have the Scriptures played in your life? What practical steps can you take to make the Scriptures more influential in your life?

4. In what way does praising God give you a proper perspective in life?

5. What is the difference between making an examination of consciousness and an examination of conscience? How can these two tools help you grow in your relationship with God?

6. What kind of role has prayer played in your life? How have you benefited from prayer? In what practical way can you increase your prayer life?

7. What area of your life do you most need to yield to God at this time?

8. Which spiritual discipline—taking time for solitude, being silent, reading the Scriptures, or praying—is most challenging for you? Why? In what practical ways can you integrate each of these disciplines into your life?

Chapter 5
Dangerous Love

Jessica was one dangerous young woman. Her attractive, even contagious, faith profoundly touched those around her. Known for her warmth, kindness, and love toward all, she had a unique ability to make people feel genuinely accepted, important, special, and loved. Because Jessica was an ideal peer minister, I wanted to figure out how to reproduce her positively dangerous qualities in all my team members.

In the hope of discovering what made Jessica so in love with Jesus, I asked: "Jessica, you've barely missed a meeting in four years. Your commitment to Jesus and to those around you has served as a model for all of us. What's your motivation? What sold you?"

Jessica's response was immediate and without a hint of hesitation. "That's easy," she said. "It was my first meeting."

"What was so special about that first meeting?" I inquired, secretly hoping that I had given a dynamic, life-changing talk that night. No such luck. She was unable to recall even the topic of the meeting, let alone the speaker. Something of greater significance had left an indelible mark on her life. She related the following experience:

Jessica was already nervous when her grandparents dropped her off and drove away that first night. When she walked in the door, she was startled by the large number of students—more than she ever dreamed and not one of whom she knew. On top of that, she soon realized these were all high school students. Someone had made a huge mistake: Jessica was only in eighth grade!

Jessica's grandparents were gone by now, and she became overwhelmed by the fact that she was younger than anyone, couldn't find a familiar face, and didn't belong at the meeting. Jessica did the only reasonable thing: she retreated to the rest room and began to cry.

Becky, a senior peer minister with just the right compassion and leadership abilities, was also in the rest room at the time. (Coincidence? Yeah, right!) When Becky asked, "Hey, are you okay?" Jessica let go another flood of tears.

Becky placed her hand on Jessica's shoulder, and the two girls talked a while. Becky's sincere care for her soothed Jessica's troubled emotions. Becky empathetically shared that she attended a different high school than almost all the other kids at these meetings and that she too had once felt like a nervous, uncomfortable outsider.

To make a long story short, Becky took Jessica by the hand, sat next to her all night, introduced her to all her senior friends (including boys!), and genuinely cared for her. She even walked Jessica to her grandfather's car afterward.

Jessica concluded her story by adding, "After that meeting I thought to myself, if Becky is an example of what it means to follow Christ and be a part of this youth group, count me in!"

Becky was one dangerous young woman. She loved Jessica in a way that vividly illustrates the beauty of the Gospel and the joy of being a member of the parish youth ministry team. Becky was fluent in the only language that Jessica would understand—the language of love.

What made the whole experience dangerous is that in direct response to Becky's gentle witness, over the next four years Jessica would reproduce in dozens (maybe hundreds) of other kids the experience of feeling welcomed and loved at youth meetings. Who knows how many other people those teens have positively affected with their new understanding of Christian hospitality and love?

(Adapted from Frank Mercadante,
Growing Teen Disciples, pp. 26–27)

We Are Called to Love Others

In chapter 3 I said, "Our level of being positively dangerous is directly proportionate to the degree to which we love God." Becky was positively dangerous to Jessica because Becky loved God first. She had spent time with the Lord and taken to heart the words of the Scriptures that call her to welcome and accept others as Christ has welcomed her (see Romans 15:7). She knew her love for God was personal but not private. As a matter of fact, Jesus says that love toward others will be the identifying characteristic of his follower (see John 13:35).

Therefore, the second characteristic of the positively dangerous person of faith is that he or she loves people. This is also the second most important commandment of the Kingdom of God—"love your neighbor as yourself" (Matthew 22:39).

Different groups of people are known for various characteristics, qualities, or customs. For example, when we think of Italians, pizza and spaghetti come to mind. Italians have built a reputation for jovial hospitality and good cooking. In the same way, Jesus says that his followers' reputation will be founded upon their heroic love for others. Love is the first thing that should come to people's minds when they hear the word *Catholic* or *Christian*.

To be positively dangerous Catholics who affect and "infect" people with God's love, we must ask God to help us accept others as Jesus does. When I was invited to that life-changing retreat in high school, the people who invited me accepted me as I was. They may not have agreed with how I was living my life at the time, but they reached out to me in love.

Too often, however, the first word that occurs to some people when they hear the term *Catholic* or *Christian* is *narrow, judgmental,* or *hypocritical.* Others often get the impression that we think we are better than they are and that we do not accept them as they are. Instead of being attracted to us and to our faith, they flee from us like they would the plague. I don't know about you, but I like being with people who make me feel better about myself. I tend to avoid being around those who look down on me. We need to ask God to give us love and acceptance for others so that we can attract others to God instead of repelling them.

If we truly loved as Jesus calls us to love, people would be clamoring at the doors of our parishes to gain entry. Love is irresistible. Love opens doors. Who doesn't want to be around people who love them? Who doesn't want to be part of a community that deeply cares for them? Genuine love is a people magnet.

> I remember a little fellow, frightened by the lightning and thunder, who called out one dark night, "Daddy, come. I'm scared." "Oh, son," the father said, "God loves you, and he'll take care of you." "I know God loves me and that he'll take care of me," the small son replied. "But right now, I want somebody who has skin on." (John Drescher, *If I Were Starting My Family Again,* p. 62)

The concrete love of Christians puts skin on God's love. God wants us to put skin on God's love for those around us.

What Is Love?

We've looked at how to love God by opening our heart to God and making our relationship with Christ our first priority. We know that if we love God, we must also love others. We may agree that accepting people and being there for them are ways to show love, but what exactly is love?

When I think of love, I don't think of words. I think of a person—my mother. She taught me the meaning of love. She put skin on God's love for me. My mother never gave me a sermon on how to love or a lecture on what love is. Instead, she very clearly and concretely illustrated love by her daily actions. In the most basic ways, my mom would deny herself things such as food, clothing, or entertainment to make sure her children's needs were fulfilled. Her life was all I needed to understand what love looks like. Her every day was a snapshot of love. She consistently demonstrated love by placing other people above her own wants and needs.

Love, in a nutshell, is a decision to take our eyes off ourselves and squarely focus them on others. Love places the interests of others above our own. Love is about giving and sacrificing on behalf of someone else.

To love and be loved are essential ingredients of life. It's a rare person who, upon the deathbed, wishes he or she had spent more time wearing the right clothes, impressing the right people, or driving the right car. In the end, life boils down to relationships—not wealth, achievement, looks, or popularity. Our love for God and for others will bring happiness to our life, and our greatest success will be that we've given many others the opportunity to know, love, and serve God in this life and to be happy with God in the next.

Ray Boltz's song "Thank You" tells the story of a man who dreams about going to heaven with his friend who helped him know Christ. When they reach heaven, his friend meets all the people he influenced for God during his lifetime, many of whom he didn't even know. The last two verses of the excerpt encourage us to love in a positively dangerous manner:

One by one they came
Far as the eye could see.
Each life somehow touched
By your generosity.
Little things that you had done,
Sacrifices made,
Unnoticed on the earth
In heaven, now proclaimed.

And I know up in heaven
You're not supposed to cry.
But I am almost sure
There were tears in your eyes
As Jesus took your hand
And you stood before the Lord.
He said, "My child, look around you.
Great is your reward."

Thank you for giving to the Lord.
I am a life that was changed.
Thank you for giving to the Lord.
I am so glad you gave.

(Ray Boltz, "Thank You," *Moments for the Heart*)

Choosing to Love

Love is much more a choice than an emotion. The greatest act
of love—Jesus' sacrificial death on the cross—is not accompanied by an exhilarating sensation. On the contrary, the stress
and anxiety of his impending passion cause Jesus to sweat
blood (a known medical condition associated with severe
anxiety). Paul challenges the faithful at Rome to "love one
another with mutual affection" and to "be ardent in spirit," that
is, fervent (Romans 12:11).

An important step to becoming a person who shares
positively dangerous love is letting go of the illusion that love
is "natural" and effortlessly flows from warm emotions. That's
true only in the movies, where love is romance accompanied

by feel-good music. Reality has no theme music in the background and often no warm and inspirational feelings launching us to heroism.

When we love, we order our thoughts, words, and actions by what is in the best interests of the other person. Love is other focused; therefore, loving others can be difficult and demanding. It is precisely because love costs so much that it holds such value.

Loving for the Benefit of Others

Allowing God to give us an accepting heart toward others, recognizing that love is mostly a choice instead of an emotion, and focusing on the needs of others are three ways we can become more positively dangerous for Christ. In addition, God calls us to use these gifts we have been given for the benefit of others.

Positively dangerous faith has less to do with the *gifts God gives us* than with how *we use these gifts* for the benefit of others and for the Kingdom of God. If we are strong, the purpose is to protect the weak. If we are intelligent, the purpose is to educate the ignorant. If we are rich, the purpose is to support the poor.

Saint Margaret of Scotland understood that her gifts were given to her for the benefit of others. She became Queen of Scotland in 1070, when she married King Malcolm. Margaret came from royalty and was well educated, intelligent, and beautiful. When she married King Malcolm, he was rough and uneducated, but her generosity and prayerfulness won him over to becoming a kind and caring man.

They were very wealthy and could have hoarded their riches for themselves, but instead they chose to share their money and food. They invited poor people to gather at the royal hall every morning and personally served them. Tradition has it that Saint Margaret would sit on a stone, near Dunfermline, where anyone in trouble could come to her for help. She fed the orphans who were brought to her. Because Saint Margaret used the gifts God had given her for the benefit of others, she has become a Christian hero, unlike so many monarchs throughout history who squandered the wealth and power entrusted to them.

Jesus is clear about the destiny of those who bury their gifts in fear (see Matthew 25:14–30). According to the Scriptures, not using the gifts entrusted to us is inexcusable. Equally detrimental is applying our gifts for our sole benefit. Some people use their physical strength to pick on weaker people, their mental intelligence to belittle those who are ignorant, or their riches to oppress people who are poor. Like Saint Margaret, those are great in the Kingdom who have used for the benefit of other people the gifts entrusted to them by God.

God has endowed all human beings with gifts to be used for the benefit of others. Think about the particular gifts God has given you. Are you using them for God's honor? Are you burying them? Are you using them to draw attention to yourself? To love in a positively dangerous manner, you need to offer back to God the gifts God has given you. When you do, you will see God using your gifts for the good of others, and you will experience the joy that comes from serving God.

Loving Through Prayer

Another way we can show love for others is by praying for them. One of the most powerful, yet underutilized, resources given to us by God is the act of intercessory prayer. Intercession, prayer on behalf of another, is a positively dangerous expression of love toward others. The following story illustrates its practical impact:

The mothers of two parish priests sat together, mending their sons' pants. One of them moaned to the other: "My poor son, Maynard—he is very discouraged at his parish. He is so down that he is thinking about asking for a transfer. Nothing goes right for him anymore." The second mother replied: "Wow, my son Elmo's pastorate is just the opposite. He's really excited about the ministry and his priesthood. His relationship with God is closer and deeper than ever." At once a revealing silence fell upon the mothers as one patched the knees and the other the seat!

In real life we're told that Saint Monica faithfully prayed for her son Augustine for over thirty years, even when it appeared that he was as far away from God as a person could wander. Her loving intercession was a key to his eventually turning back to God. Augustine is now esteemed as one of the wisest and most beloved saints of the Church.

Loving the Hard-to-Love

The youth group meeting had ended earlier in the afternoon, and I was doing the last bit of cleanup before heading home. John was the only person left in a group of about forty high school teens. John was an outcast from a family of outcasts. His older brother and sister shared his lot among their peers. The kids in the community unfairly branded his entire family.

Prior to my conversion, I too saw John as somewhat of a leper. Overweight, dressed like a janitor, and enrolled in the lower-level classes, John was ridiculed, picked on, and pushed around by plenty of people in his high school. His few friends shared his sad fate. John was a newcomer in the youth group, and the other teens were pleasant to him, but no one was a friend to him beyond the meetings.

I finished the last of my cleanup and told John I had to lock the door. "Okay," he meekly replied. As we walked outside, I saw that my car was the only one left in the parking lot. I turned to John and asked, "How are you getting home?"

"I was just going to walk," John replied, looking me in the eyes long enough to make me feel uncomfortable. I knew that John lived several miles away, and I immediately felt the pressure to offer him a ride.

What went on in my mind during the next few moments changed my life. I remember thinking to myself: "Oh, no! I've got to drive John home!" Being at a meeting where John was present was one thing. Driving through town with him in the front seat of my car was entirely another matter. I was hesitant to offer this kid a ride. I didn't want to be seen in public with John. I was afraid of what others might think. I looked at him as being inferior to me.

At that moment I was internally confronted with my own arrogance. I could sense Jesus speaking to my heart—and it was a strong word. "Who do you think you are? I love John like I love you. I died for John like I died for you."

I swallowed hard and forced the words out of my mouth, "John, I'll give you a ride home." John, looking surprised and relieved, replied: "Really? Thanks!" I am embarrassed to admit that the ride was long and uncomfortable for me, but it changed my life.

Jesus gravitates toward people on earth who are like John. He reaches out to poor people. God calls us to love people who seem to be unlovable, to befriend those who are unpopular, to risk speaking with those who are ostracized. Positively dangerous love is not selective but inclusive, and its impact is often life-changing for those who have previously been so frequently rejected.

Think of a person like John in your life, and pray for him or her. Ask God for the grace to love that person as Christ would. Pray for an opportunity to bring Christ's love into that person's life. Be ready to seize the moment when the opportunity comes. You may see the fruit of your prayers and active love, or you may not, but be assured that God is working through your prayer and action.

Loving Our Family

Often the place we think least about being positively dangerous is in our own home, among our own family members. Few of us would deny that we deeply love our family, yet, ironically, they often get the worst of us (probably because we know they will take it and still love us). How many friends would we have if we treated them like we do our brothers or sisters? Also, it is easy to take our parents for granted and show very little appreciation toward them. In reality, our home should be the first place where we exercise dangerous love—not the last. Our parents and siblings should see the greatest evidence of our faith.

In the classic movie *The Wizard of Oz,* Dorothy temporarily loses her family and comes to recognize that even though she lives with imperfect people, "there's no place like home." May we not have to lose any family members to appreciate the gift that each one of them is to us.

Let's talk about some of the ways we can show positively dangerous love and faith at home.

Loving Our Parents

One way to show love to our parents is to do more than they ask us to do rather than the least amount possible. Or if we really want to freak them out, we can do something they didn't even ask us to do. A real jaw dropper would be to thank them for all the hard work they do for us! Think, "What could I do for Mom that would really help her?" "What's one thing I could do for Dad that would show him that I care about him?" Often we can express our love for God in the little things in life. Taking out the garbage, doing the dishes, filling up the gas tank, or helping with the laundry may be the most loving thing we can do for God today. Wanting to be a positively dangerous person of faith begins at home.

Loving Our Siblings

Deanna and her sister Samantha never got along very well. Samantha, who was two years older than Deanna, would often pick on her younger sister, as older sisters do sometimes. They didn't have a lot in common and were often competitive. Although they loved each other, a wall of resentment rose between them over the years. They were much more sisters than friends.

During her junior year, Samantha attended a parish retreat weekend that woke her up spiritually. She came home excited about her faith and claimed that her life had changed.

Samantha was nicer to Deanna, but Deanna was initially skeptical. She had seen others come home with retreat highs that lasted a week or two.

Over the next several months, however, Samantha stopped saying mean things to her sister, helped her with homework, and even expressed interest in the details of Deanna's life. For the first time, they were actually talking like real friends. Deanna couldn't help but note the difference in Samantha. With each passing day, her sister's warmth thawed Deanna's skepticism. Maybe Samantha's faith was real after all!

Then one day everything changed. Samantha came home from a friend's house in a foul mood and got all over Deanna. Before long Samantha snapped off some venomous words—like a replay of the past. Angry and annoyed, Deanna stormed to her room. She knew all along that her sister's "conversion" was too good to be true and would never last. She settled back into her familiar skepticism.

Soon there was a gentle knock at Deanna's door by a broken Samantha. With tears running down her cheeks, she said: "Deanna, I had a terrible day at school, but it is no excuse for the way I treated you. You don't deserve what I said. I want you to know how deeply sorry I am for what I said to you. Please forgive me."

That winter Deanna attended the same retreat weekend that had changed her sister's life. She was deeply touched by God. On the following spring retreat, Deanna became a member of the peer ministry team and shared her faith journey with a roomful of teenagers. She told them how her sister's love toward her convinced her of the reality of God's love. Deanna and Samantha became committed to their faith, their parish youth ministry, and each other. Samantha loved her sister Deanna with a positively dangerous love—so danger-ously contagious that Deanna caught the same life-changing faith.

We should exercise positively dangerous love at home. If we love our brothers and sisters, we should want to give them our greatest gift—our faith in Jesus Christ. The way we treat them can become a crucial bridge to Jesus instead of a barrier. Our siblings need to experience firsthand that our love for Christ means that we love them too. If our love for God doesn't affect our love for our brothers and sisters at home, we are missing the boat. With God's help we can become more loving and, like Samantha, be a bridge toward Christ for them.

Some Final Thoughts

From the rejected people we meet in society to our daily acquaintances to our family, God calls us to love. This love is a decision that we express by accepting other people, sacrificially doing both small and heroic acts for them, using our God-entrusted gifts for their benefit, and praying for them. As we grow closer to Christ, God's love fills our heart and spills over into every relationship in our life. The more love we give away, the more love we will receive from God, and we will experience the joy of blessing other peoples' lives.

Questions for Reflection and Discussion

1. In the opening story of this chapter, Becky's positively dangerous example makes a big difference in Jessica's life. If possible, share an experience when someone has reached out to you and made a difference in your life.

2. The second characteristic of positively dangerous people of faith is that they love other people. Why is loving others so important to the Christian life?

3. Has someone in your life put "skin" on God's love for you? If so, what has this person done?

4. Are there people in your life who need to experience God's love? If so, what is one way you can put "skin" on God's love for them?

5. To say that love is much more a choice than an emotion is foreign to the message of today's culture. How does contemporary culture define love? Do you agree that love is more a choice than an emotion? Why or why not?

6. What gifts has God given to you? What is one way you can use them to benefit others?

7. Time given in prayer on behalf of other people is a concrete way to love them. Think of a person (or a group) for whom God may wish you to pray; make a plan to do so.

8. In your life is there someone you consider less than yourself or whom you find difficult to love? If so, in what ways do you think you can be more loving to this person?

9. The love you have for God needs to be expressed at home. You can show love for your parent(s) in three ways: do more than they ask you to do, do something they haven't asked you to do, and express appreciation for what they do for you. Identify one or two ways you can express love to your parent(s) this week.

10. In what ways are you a bridge to Christ for your siblings? How can you strengthen this bridge?

Chapter 6
Be Real!

Jenny sat nervously, her thin, brown hair framing her hollowed cheeks and sunken, brown eyes. She shivered and pulled her too large coat more closely to her weary body. She had a million questions running through her mind, the least of which was why she was almost "forced" by the hospital's staff to be at this meeting. She risked a glance and noted that many of the people gathered were overweight—the disfigurement that she feared the most. Others seemed "normal" and physically fit, something she couldn't say for herself at this point. Even amidst the diversity, she saw one thing they had in common— they were smiling, laughing together, and genuinely comfortable with one another. How long had it been since she was comfortable with any group of people? Jenny didn't even seem to "fit" with herself.

Jenny's musings were cut short when everyone gathered around the table. The room became painfully quiet, and Jenny wondered what would come next. A young man in his thirties, whom she deemed to be the leader, began: "Welcome to the Sunday night meeting of Overeaters Anonymous. My name is Joe, and I'm your leader for this meeting. Are there any other compulsive overeaters, anorexics, or bulimics here besides me?" All hands (except Jenny's) were raised, unashamedly.

Next Joe asked whether anyone was here for the first, second, or third time. Jenny slowly raised her hand and felt exposed, like a deer in headlights. She told her first name and was asked for nothing more. Everyone joyfully welcomed her as though she were attending a Christmas party instead of a twelve-step group. She managed a faint, "Thank you," and then they returned to the task at hand. As Joe continued to read his scripted sheet, one sentence jumped out at Jenny: "It is weakness, not strength, that binds us together and somehow gives us the power to do what we cannot do alone." Jenny had spent so much of her teenage life trying to hide her weakness that the idea of weakness bringing a group together was unimaginable.

Jenny listened intently as the meeting changed pace. The group members read a few sentences from the "Big Book" of Alcoholics Anonymous and then spoke honestly about their life. A young woman named Kim shared how this past week had been a real struggle for her. Kim bravely admitted that one night she had eaten so much that she could barely move and had secretly relieved herself by vomiting. With teary eyes and a quivering voice, Kim stated her belief that bringing her secret into the open would help her take the necessary steps to make a better decision next time. Kim received no reprimands from the group, only sincere eyes and listening ears.

As the personal stories continued, Jenny began to relax. She heard others tell of their struggles with food and body image. She realized for the first time that she was not alone. Others understood exactly how she felt and what would lead a sixteen-year-old who seemed to "have it all together" to Saint

Joseph Hospital's eating disorder unit. Their honesty, their willingness to say it like it is, and their genuine acceptance of one another's weaknesses gave Jenny the courage to tell some of her story. In spite of being unsure of her future with this group, Jenny felt connected, and this feeling made her want to come back.

Although Jenny experienced authenticity from these group members, twelve-step groups are not the only place to experience this third quality of being positively dangerous to others. Our parish communities in general, and youth ministry in particular, will attract many believers if we offer this quality of authenticity. Jesus Christ invites all followers to grow in authenticity—to be honest and sincere with one another, to be themselves, and to accept others as they are. This quality of authenticity is so important because it draws other people in, helps them feel connected, and opens the door for a meaningful relationship. Authenticity gives others permission to be themselves, warts and all. When we are authentic with others, they will want to be around us. They will trust us, and this bond may be the bridge that eventually leads them to Christ.

Defining Authenticity

Authenticity is being real and genuine. The authentic person relieves others of the burden of peeling away layers of masks before they can find the real person underneath. The authentic person practices the *WYSIWYG* principle: What You See Is What You Get. We are who we are, whether on stage or off.

When we describe something as authentic, we mean that it is the *real deal.* Items that are real always have greater value than ones that are not. Real gold is more valuable than fool's gold. Diamonds are worth far more than cubic zirconium. An original Picasso is much more valuable than the print we buy at the mall. Having a relationship with a person who is honest, sincere, and genuine is worth far more than being with a fake.

I had a friend I admired in college. He was committed to Jesus and willing to give his life for the cause of Christ. He graduated and left to share the Gospel in one of the most dangerous regions in the world. His courage was very inspiring, but I never personally connected with him or felt close to him. He never revealed the real Dan—his struggles, insecurities, and fears. Instead Dan focused on the cause of Christ and the need to reach the world with the Gospel. In reality, Dan was hiding his true self behind "doing the work of the Church." He was forfeiting his opportunity to connect intimately with others. Now that I look back, Dan was never close to anyone; he was a loner. We all admired him from a distance but were too wary to get close to him.

Without authenticity we cannot experience human intimacy. Like Dan, sometimes we're afraid to be "real" or authentic because we fear our struggles may set a bad example for others. Mistakenly we may think that to be positively dangerous, we have to lead people to believe that we are somehow above them. We may reason that if people knew our struggles, weaknesses, and shortcomings, we would lose our moral and spiritual credibility. Ironically the opposite is true. Our struggles give us credibility in the eyes of others. For example, a person who has been a victim of a violent crime is going to be a much more credible source on the importance of "forgiving our enemies" than someone who has no enemies. Also, when we are honest about our life, we free those around us to be honest about theirs. When we peel off our mask, others tend to remove theirs.

What Makes a Person Authentic?

When I consider the authentic people I know in my life, I realize that they possess certain qualities, such as sincerity, honesty, and acceptance. I also notice that they lack three other traits. They aren't judgmental; they aren't anxious about being human; they aren't afraid of being themselves, no matter what group of people they hang out with. What helps such people be honest, sincere, and accepting, but *not* judgmental, anxious, and afraid? I can answer that question by examining Jesus' life more closely, for he is the most authentic person I know.

First, Jesus is absolutely convinced of the Father's love for him. He believes, even in the midst of the heart wrenching and painful circumstances of the cross, that God loves him. Knowing with certainty that God loves him doesn't take the pain away when his arms are nailed to the cross, but this knowledge does allow Jesus to choose the cross. Jesus knows that because God loves him, God will get him through it. Jesus knows that because God loves him, a loving purpose lies behind the suffering.

The same is true for us: God loves us, no matter what our circumstances are. Jesus tells us in plain language, "As the Father has loved me, so I have loved you" (John 15:9). Saint Paul assures us that God's love is always present: "For I am convinced that neither death, nor life, nor angels, nor rulers, nor things present, nor things to come, nor powers, nor height, nor depth, nor anything else in all creation, will be able to separate us from the love of God in Christ Jesus our Lord" (Romans 8:38–39). This sentence sums up anything that can happen to us! God's love for us is real and always present in our life.

A priest whom I admire often says that God calls us *beloved*. Until we believe we are the beloved of God, we spend our life desperately trying to prove our worth. We stress out trying to get straight A's, fearing that a B will shatter our perfect image. We look for love from the girl or boy of our dreams, and when we don't get it, we believe that we're somehow defective. We try to prove our worth by fitting in—sometimes with any group that will include us, even if it means harming ourselves with alcohol or drugs. Until we begin to believe the absolute truth that God really loves us, we are restless and spend the majority of our time trying to prove our worth.

Sometimes we believe that God loves us if we are "good." As long as we try hard to serve God and to please our parents, teachers, and friends, we are loved. But when we blow it, we feel that we are not as lovable. Nowhere in the Scriptures will we find that God loves us because we are "good." When we fall, we are given a chance to turn away from our sin and back to God. When we hurt others, we can ask them to forgive us. When we make mistakes, we can learn from them. We are not meant to live our "good" life apart from God. We *need* God to rescue us from our sin and selfishness, and there is no shame in that! This is precisely why Jesus has come into the world—to save us! The Creator has given us free will to accept or to reject God's love, but we cannot earn God's love.

If we are not convinced of God's love for us (which often does take time), we can adopt some practical steps. In our daily prayer time, we can ask God to help us believe that we are loved. We can also read Scripture passages that assure us of God's love.

If you're not sure how to find passages about God's love, consult the "Life and Faith Issues" section of *The Catholic Youth Bible* for specific Scripture passages that address the subject. Also, you can look up "God's love" in a concordance of the Bible and find several references. Perhaps you know some people who seem to understand a lot about the Scriptures; ask them if they can show you where to look. Filling your mind with the truth that God loves you will combat the lie that you are not loved or that you are loved only when you are "good."

Free to Be Yourself

As you come to live in the security of God's love, you become more authentic because you are free to be yourself. It is also good to be inspired by others, especially as you seek to develop the character traits and virtues they have mastered. The lives of the saints serve as an inspiration for countless

Catholics. However, being authentic means being the *you* God created and is calling you to be. The Lord wants you to be uniquely you—not a carbon copy of someone else. You can take imitation too far and lose your authentic self and God's unique call.

God created each of us uniquely and has a special plan for us. We will never experience this plan if we live our life trying to be someone else, like a screwdriver that wants to be a hammer. A screwdriver is never meant for the tasks of a hammer. Driving nails by the force of a screwdriver handle is ineffective and frustrating at best.

One of the most exciting and freeing aspects of life is discovering who God made us to be and what God is calling us to do. To discover this call, we must embrace and love the person we are. Authenticity begins with accepting ourselves as good. We agree with the Lord: after creating humankind in God's image, "God saw everything that he had made, and indeed, it was very good" (Genesis 1:31).

Once we begin to cling to the truth that God loves us and has already created us as "good," we can be comfortable within ourselves and with any group of people. Jesus is the same person with the Pharisees as he is with the lepers. He welcomes the company of children, and contrary to the cultural norms of his day, he treats women with dignity and often speaks with them.

We too can be ourselves. We don't have to be social marionettes, manipulated by other people. We can allow our actions to come from the heart and choose to live as God would have us, not as others expect.

Judging Others

As we come to accept God's personal love, we can also believe that God loves others just as much. Our Creed says that Jesus "will come again to judge the living and the dead." God the Father designates Jesus as the judge of all; we have not been given that job! Authentic people have the ability to accept others and don't feel the need to put them down. When Jesus is walking the earth, he doesn't focus on judging others but on bringing God's love and truth to them so that they can be free from the bondage of sin. In the dramatic Gospel story of the woman caught in adultery, Jesus tells her persecutors, "Let anyone among you who is without sin be the first to throw a stone at her" (John 8:7). This advice goes for us as well.

If we're honest, many of us are tempted to judge others—somehow I feel better about myself if I can find all of Megan's or Josh's flaws. Even when we begin to live our life more for God, we can be tempted to judge whether we are more "spiritual" than someone else. Jesus cannot be clearer about his feelings on this subject (see Luke 7:36–50). When we give up our judgment seat and join the rest of the human family, we will be much happier and far more authentic.

To practice authenticity we can pray daily for an accepting heart. We can ask God to help us see others and ourselves through God's eyes. Just being aware that judging others isn't our job is helpful. We can remind ourselves that there are no teacher's pets in the Kingdom; all are equally loved. We are not above or below others; we're on the same path.

When judgmental thoughts come at us like fastballs, we can bat them away with the truth that it is not our job to judge, and we can pray for that person instead of dwelling on his or her negative qualities. When we find ourselves sitting in judgment of others, we should stop and ask for God's forgiveness. Bringing this sin to the sacrament of Reconciliation will help us receive more grace to overcome it.

A note of caution: although we are not to judge other people, as Catholics we are called to stand up for Gospel values. For example, it is not our job to judge a friend who is considering an abortion, but it is our duty to help her recognize that an abortion will take the life of her baby, which is a grave sin. We are called to reach out and help her as much as we can, to guide her to get the help she needs so that she does not make the wrong choice. There is a difference between judging a person and knowing that an action is clearly wrong.

In the Gospel account of the woman caught in adultery, Jesus loves the woman but calls her to walk away from the sin in her life. He does not say, "You're a good person, so your sin doesn't matter." He loves her as a person, forgives her, and speaks the truth to her so that she can change.

Why is it so tough to be real? Because being real is all we've got—and people may not like who we are. Yet, being real also makes us approachable. It connects us to other people and invites them to be authentic. Authenticity may be the very quality that enables us to "infect" others with the love and the acceptance of Christ.

1. On a scale measuring your authenticity, from one to ten (one is being a "fake," and ten is being "real" with others), where would you place yourself?

2. Why does authenticity open the door to another person's heart? What can you do to be more authentic with others?

3. Authentic people are not judgmental, anxious about being human, or afraid of being themselves, no matter what group of people they hang out with. Do you experience difficulty in any of these areas? If so, explain.

4. If your ability to be authentic is not closely linked to your belief in God's unconditional love for you, you will spend a lot of time trying to gain approval in other ways. Do you find yourself seeking approval? If so, how?

5. You can accept or reject God's love, but you cannot earn it. In what ways do you try to earn God's love?

6. Judging others comes easily to most people; today's culture accepts it as normal behavior. Why do you think Jesus speaks so strongly to his followers against being judgmental? What difference does it make in your life and in the life of others whether or not you are judgmental?

7. Tolerance is the highest value in contemporary society. Although you are not to judge a person's heart, you are called to stand firm for the values of the Kingdom of God, which are often contrary to the world around you. In what one way may God be calling you to stand firm in a conviction that goes against society's tolerant attitude?

8. Do you find yourself acting differently with various groups of people? If so, why do you think you do this?

Chapter 7 Walking the Talk

Several years ago I took a group of teens to a summer conference. I also had the joy of bringing along my pastor, a wonderful and godly man. During the young men's session, we were sitting on a hard concrete floor in a large auditorium in the blistering heat of early afternoon. I huddled the guys and my pastor around me just prior to the afternoon speaker.

"Guys, I know what it's like after lunch. I feel it too. We're tired and would like nothing better than a nap. It's a challenge to listen to another speaker; however, please try to sit up in a respectful position, make eye contact with the presenter, and listen to the best of your ability. Now, if your mind can't hold on to the content, I understand, but at least maintain a respectful posture. No speaker likes to look out at a comatose audience blissfully snoring through his heartfelt message. I know from personal experience—it's not very inspiring! So just be polite, okay, guys?"

Our speaker began—and sure enough, his style was reminiscent of the most skilled anesthesiologist. A spirit of narcolepsy invaded the room as he droned on in a monotonous tone.

My students were getting a little restless, but they were all holding to an attentive posture. My pastor, however, slipped into a more comfortable position, his back flat to the floor and his knees raised. At least his eyes were open, I assured myself as I observed his glazed, blank staring at the ceiling. All my students looked at me and smirked.

A few minutes later, as our speaker's words poured out with the dynamism of cold molasses, my pastor's knees collapsed to the floor. My entire group carefully observed him and then looked at me. He was now lying flat on the floor, with his eyes half open. An interesting dynamic then took place. My students obviously wanted to be as comfortable and carefree as their pastor, but they were wrestling with the weight of my earlier instructions. They were torn because I said to pay attention, but he was not paying attention, and he was their pastor!

Five more minutes passed by, and "sleeping beauty" was flat on his back, eyes tightly closed, and breathing very heavily! By the end of the talk, guess what position my students were in? If you guess the attentive one described by my earlier words to them, you are wrong. They followed what was modeled.

(Adapted from Frank Mercadante,
Growing Teen Disciples, pp. 31–32)

Although the story is humorous, the fact is that how we conduct ourselves will always weigh more heavily than our words. Our examples will serve as our most compelling sermons (see 2 Corinthians 3:2). People are influenced by what they see us doing. People who grow up in families where they have been abused as children, or where one parent beats the other, grow up learning that violence is normal behavior. It is impossible for people to operate outside their own knowledge base and experiences. As humans we do what we know and what is comfortable to us.

What we see is often what we do; therefore, before we can bravely proclaim our faith, we must boldly live our faith. Ralph Waldo Emerson once said: "Don't *say* things. What you *are* stands over you the while, and thunders so that I cannot hear what you say to the contrary" (*Letters and Social Aims,* p. 96).

Defining Integrity

The fourth characteristic of positively dangerous people of faith is integrity. Authenticity is about being real. Integrity is about being whole. Authenticity is being honest about who we are. Integrity is being complete—inner beliefs match outward actions. Authenticity means we are who we are, no matter whom we are with or what we are doing. Integrity means being true to the Good News we represent, even when others are not looking. Integrity is the opposite of hypocrisy. Integrity is living in agreement with our convictions; hypocrisy is living in opposition to our beliefs.

Integrity measures our stated beliefs against our demonstrated behavior. If we boast with six feet of words but only demonstrate six inches of action, we lack integrity. Six feet of beliefs balanced by six feet of consistent conduct is pure integrity.

Getting Respect as a Youth

The comedian Rodney Dangerfield has made a career with a single phrase: "I get no respect!" Most young people can easily identify with that phrase. Many teens feel they are not respected or taken seriously by adults. Things weren't much different in the early Church. The Apostle Paul, while mentoring a young man named Timothy, encourages him to be the leader God is calling him to be. Knowing that because of Timothy's age, older believers might not respect him (see 1 Timothy 4:12), Paul gives Timothy a road map to credibility.

The best way to gain the attention and the trust of adults (and of peers) is through your exemplary character. When you set the example and illustrate to those around you what it means to be like Christ, *you will be respected.* To be positively dangerous, you must earn the respect of others by raising the bar in personal holiness. I have seen teens apply their natural idealism to living the Gospel in such an exemplary manner that adults not only recognize their leadership but also are inspired to give more of themselves to Christ in response.

Be an Example

One day a proud and pompous parish deacon was teaching a sixth-grade religious education class. He was attempting to teach the children the importance of living a Christian life. "Why do people call me a Christian?" he confidently inquired of the class. After an awkward silence, one forthright young boy answered, "Maybe it's because they don't know you."

Our example is our sermon to the world. A positive, consistent example will draw interest from others. A negative, inconsistent pattern will only disillusion others, making them skeptical of our faith. Saint Paul sets the standard for leaders (both young and old) when he confidently writes to the Corinthian believers, "Be imitators of me, as I am of Christ" (1 Corinthians 11:1). Paul is saying, in effect, "Imitating me can lead you to Christlikeness."

Young leaders need to take Paul's challenge seriously. Can you say to others, "Imitate me—it will lead you to Jesus"? Certainly none of us is perfect, but do we live in a manner that accurately represents Jesus? Is our life consistent with the teachings of Christ, or is it full of convenient compromises?

To be positively dangerous, to launch an epidemic of faith, we need to embrace Paul's standard. In a time when leadership scandals threaten to destroy the credibility of our Church, we need to raise up a new standard of leadership. We need to live a holy life. Saying, "I am only a teenager; what do I have to offer?" is no excuse. Remember that God thinks a lot! God uses young people in heroic ways throughout the centuries (Jeremiah, Timothy, Mary, and Joan of Arc, to name a few).

Paul encourages young Timothy to define the standard by setting "the believers an example in speech and conduct, in love, in faith, in purity" (1 Timothy 4:12). Christians who do this live with integrity. Let's look at each of Paul's five examples in greater detail.

Example in Speech

"Sticks and stones may break my bones, but words will never hurt me." It's a nice thought, but why do most of us still painfully remember the ugly names and stinging words that others have carelessly shared with us? For some the reckless words of others have seared and branded their self-image. Every day they look in the mirror and see a distorted image that has been carefully contoured by the heartless words of others. Every day they fight to free themselves from hounding scripts that scream: "I am stupid!" "I am ugly!" "I am a loser!" "I am a nobody!" Words are extremely powerful; the mouth can be a weapon of mass destruction.

It is easy to be careless with our words. The Epistle of James warns us of the power of the tongue: "How great a forest is set ablaze by a small fire! And the tongue is a fire" (3:5–6). James also warns us of the duplicity of our tongue: "With it we bless the Lord and Father, and with it we curse those who are made in the likeness of God. From the same mouth come blessing and cursing. My brothers and sisters, this ought not to be so" (3:9–10).

Only one standard should exist for what comes out of the mouth—saying the things that will build others up. As Paul says, "Let no evil talk come out of your mouths, but only what is useful for building up, as there is need, so that your words may give grace to those who hear" (Ephesians 4:29). Weigh your words; consider whether they are motivated by love or serve a self-centered intention. Use your words to encourage, support, strengthen, and build up.

During my late teens, I attended a large gathering of Christians. A woman I had never met before prayed with me during one session. Afterward she looked me in the eye and proclaimed, "Young man, God's hand is upon you, and God is going to use you in great ways."

My average life ended that day. I believed her—even though I was an unlikely candidate for God to use. I was an average guy, with average grades, looking at an average future. That woman's uplifting words caused me to believe that God could use an ordinary person like me in extraordinary ways. To this day I thank God for that woman, whom I had never met before and haven't seen since. Her encouraging words helped change my destiny.

Gossip. A Native American woman once shared with her neighbors some juicy rumors about another woman in the village. Later she found out that what she had reported was not true. Feeling bad, she went to the wise man in her village to see what she could do to make things right. The wise man instructed her to go home and slaughter a chicken, pluck the feathers, place them in a bag, and then come back, scattering the feathers throughout the village on her way.

The woman did as she was told. When she reported back, the wise man gave her one last set of instructions: "Now go the way you came, and gather back all the feathers you have scattered."

She objected, "But by now the wind has blown the feathers throughout the village and beyond!"

The wise man concluded, "And so have your careless words."

As attractive as it may be, gossip never builds others up but almost always damages people beyond repair. A thief can reimburse a victim after stealing, but like a murderer—who cannot give back the life taken—the gossiper can rarely undo the damage of an assassinated reputation. Passing on negative information about others is never the right thing to do. You can also be sure that the person who talks to you about others will talk to others about you.

Profanity. Swearing can become so commonplace that we fail to realize what we are saying; yet using it cheapens our witness. Profanity almost always reduces our credibility in the eyes of others. Most people don't associate its use with the serious follower of Jesus. Furthermore, telling others dirty or off-color jokes has the same negative effect. Often the little differences in our speech set us apart from others.

Our external words are clues to our internal character. What's in the well comes out in the water. What's in the tree comes out in the fruit. What's in our heart comes out of our mouth. In essence, our words advertise our soul. Before saying anything about another person, we should **THINK**. If the answer to any of the questions below is no, it is probably best not to say anything.

- Is it **True**?
- Is it **Helpful**?
- Is it **Inspiring**?
- Is it **Necessary**?
- Is it **Kind**?

Example in Conduct

While shaking her pastor's hand one Sunday after Mass, a gray-haired old woman who regularly attended church said: "Father, that was a wonderful homily indeed. Everything you said applies to someone I know."

Like the old woman, we can easily get caught up in the shortcomings of others while forgetting our own. The Apostle Paul challenges us to focus on our own life and to be an example of Christian conduct (see Philippians 1:27).

When the Apostle Peter is condemned to die on account of his faith, he vigorously protests against being crucified like Jesus. He is not a coward and afraid to suffer and die. On the contrary, he tells his executioners that he is not worthy to die in the same position as his Lord. He chooses to be crucified upside down!

Peter understands the honor of being a disciple of Jesus. He wants to live and die in a manner worthy of his Lord. Not only is Peter not going to compromise, he is going to take the high road. If we, like Peter, want to be positively dangerous, we must not compromise our conduct. We must take the moral high road.

Talking about the do's and don'ts of conduct "worthy of the Gospel" almost diminishes the beauty and nobility of our call. It is like asking a close friend for detailed instructions on exactly how to love and then following them in a lifeless and mechanical manner. A much richer road of expression is to order all our thoughts, words, and behaviors by the desire to love and respect our friend.

The same is true of our relationship with the Lord. Our behavior should stem from our desire to bring our Lord honor and to express our deep love for Jesus. Would we consider doing things like getting drunk at a party, being disrespectful to a teacher, or cheating on a test? Absolutely not. Such activities would not only dishonor our Lord, our Catholic faith, and our Christian community but also place a barrier preventing those around us from becoming interested in our faith. Instead our conduct should be an irresistible magnetic force that attracts others to Jesus.

Example in Love

Randy didn't look much like a churchgoer. He came to Mass late, dressed in tattered jeans and a T-shirt riddled with Swiss-cheese holes and wearing no shoes. His long, disheveled hair and scruffy, unshaven face matched the roughness of his attire. Randy attended a nearby college, where he had recently experienced a conversion while on retreat. Churchgoing was new to him. The packed suburban church was primarily made up of wealthy and conservative parishioners.

Randy waltzed in during the Gospel reading. Being tardy, he could not find a place to sit. With each step he captured the attention of more of the congregation. People were getting more uncomfortable as he searched each pew, seeking a place to sit. With all eyes upon him, Randy walked to the front of the sanctuary and slumped in the aisle, taking a seat on the cold tile floor. Every eye was on Randy. Then, from the back, Mr. Ruettiger, a senior usher, began making his way toward the front. The Gospel reading was just about over, but no one was listening. The only thing anyone could hear was the clicking of Mr. Ruettiger's wooden cane as he slowly edged toward Randy.

Everyone knew what was about to happen. No one could blame Mr. Ruettiger, a man in his seventies who couldn't possibly be expected to understand the dress and behavior of this young college student. Nevertheless, everyone was tense and nervous. As the Gospel reading ended, all remained silent and standing, craning and shifting to get a better view of the coming confrontation. Even the presiding priest paused in anticipation.

Mr. Ruettiger arrived at the feet of Randy and dropped his cane. The loud echo stunned every curious onlooker. Then, slowly and painfully, Mr. Ruettiger lowered himself to the hard tile floor and sat down next to Randy. Mr. Ruettiger warmly smiled and patted Randy on the back. He remained at Randy's side so he wouldn't have to sit alone. The entire congregation was deeply touched by Mr. Ruettiger's kindness and love. The priest began his homily: "What I am about to preach you may never remember. What you just witnessed you will never forget."

Being an example of love means treating others like royalty. Be known as one of the kindest, most caring, and most giving people in your school. Remember that love is the distinguishing mark of Jesus' disciples. Reach out to those who sit alone at the lunch table and who put you off by their personality, behavior, or manner of dress. Love those whose social status might diminish your own for associating with them. Love your enemies. Be an example of love.

Example in Faith

The Great Blondin was an incredible circus performer whose acrobatic feats amazed and delighted the crowds surrounding him. No acrobatic challenge was too extreme for the Great Blondin.

He once traversed a thin steel cable stretched across the rapidly churning waters of Niagara Falls. In high winds and without the security of a safety net, Blondin walked across the tightwire. The crowd became more excited as he effortlessly ran, even danced, across the thin wire.

As if that weren't enough, one day Blondin crossed the wire while pushing a wheelbarrow loaded with bricks. While the crowd was cheering in delight, Blondin yelled, "Do you believe I can cross while pushing a man in this wheelbarrow?"

The crowd was utterly convinced—with not a dissenter in the group—as they raised their hands in approval.

"Then," challenged Blondin, "who will be that man?"

The crowd went silent as their arms dropped to their sides. Not a soul volunteered. Not one of Blondin's "believers" was willing to entrust his life into Blondin's hands. (Adapted from Frank Mercadante, *Small Group Leader's Guide for Teens,* pp. 8–9)

Faith is all about trust. Faith is about putting our life on the line and trusting that our Lord will take care of us. Being an example of faith means that we live obediently according to the call and the commandments of Christ, trusting that our Lord will work all things together for the good (see Romans 8:28), even if the situation doesn't look so good at the moment. Faith depends on the trustworthiness of Almighty God, not on circumstances or situations.

Seeking to be an example of integrity will be costly at times. We may lose friends, be misunderstood, or be ridiculed. We may even seem worse for it, but we can respect ourselves and be confident that God will not abandon us when we seek to do the Lord's will.

Example in Purity

When we read the description "pure," we think 100 percent of the real thing: "pure, all-beef hot dogs," "pure, 100 percent maple syrup," "pure, 24-karat gold." Advertisers are well aware that "pure" sells. No brand advertises in big, bold characters: "mostly pure" or "only 10 percent filler." Pure means no fillers, no added substances of a lesser value, no dilution of the real thing. When Paul tells Timothy to be an example in purity, he is encouraging him to be single-minded, wholly devoted, and 100 percent committed to the things of God. The term Paul uses almost always connotes pure in a moral sense: a totally, fully, completely, unreservedly, uncompromisingly, all-out, 24/7 commitment to Jesus and his way of life.

Purity begins in the mind and means filling it with wholesome, positive, and worthy things. Our devotion to Christ can waver when we begin to feed our mind and imagination with images, words, and music primarily rooted in this world. Being an example of purity means discerning the kind of media we choose to listen to or watch. A general rule of thumb is to ask, "Would I share this magazine, book, Web site, music, movie, or television show with Jesus?" If we would be uncomfortable sharing an activity with Jesus, we had best avoid that activity.

When we compromise on purity, we become distracted from following Jesus. We reduce Jesus' influence and lordship in our life because our heart is divided. Over time the Lord's voice in our life becomes dull and faint, and God is unable to use us. The final result is that we reduce our positively dangerous factor down to nothing. We become cottage-cheese Catholics.

If you are young, adults might not initially take you seriously. If you seek to be an example in speech, conduct, love, faith, and purity, people will take notice. You will be, without a doubt, positively dangerous.

Questions for Reflection and Discussion

1. Do you agree with the saying, "Actions speak louder than words"? If so, what is one of the main "messages" of your life?

2. Integrity means being true to the Good News you represent, even when others are not looking. How does integrity apply to your life right now?

3. You are called to be an example in speech: "Let no evil talk come out of your mouths, but only what is useful for building up, as there is need, so that your words may give grace to those who hear" (Ephesians 4:29). How does your life measure up to this Scripture passage? What one thing can you ask God to help you change to be more in line with this standard?

4. Many people consider gossiping about others as normal speech, and much of the conversation among teenagers (and adults) is gossip—saying things about others that you wouldn't say if they were present. Why do people spend so much time gossiping? Why do the Scriptures state that this type of conversation is so harmful?

5. What percentage of your conversation time do you spend either gossiping or listening to gossip? What can you do to make your communication with others more positive and encouraging?

6. The Scriptures state that God does not want you to use profane words. How challenging is this advice for you? How much of a change is required to remove profanity from your speech? Why is this important to do?

7. Your behavior should stem from a desire to bring the Lord honor and to express your deep love for Jesus. Consider your life. To honor and to express love for the Lord, do you need to change any areas?

8. God calls you and Timothy to be examples of love, which means to reach out to the unlovable, the ones no one wants to sit with, those who are made fun of the most. How do you show this kind of love? What, if anything, needs to change in your heart so that you are willing to extend Christ's love to all people?

9. To live by faith, you need to believe that Christ will take care of you and work all things for the good in your life as you seek to follow him. On a scale of one to ten (one is not believing this truth, and ten is fully believing in Christ's care), where do you place yourself at this time? Explain.

10. How do you evaluate what media you read, listen to, and watch? What do you think about evaluating books, movies, television shows, magazines and music by the following standard: "Would I share this magazine, book, Web site, music, movie, or television show with Jesus?" Are you willing to adopt this standard for your life? Why or why not?

11. Which one of the five areas—speech, love, conduct, faith, and purity—is the most challenging for you? Why? Take some time to ask God to help you begin to make changes in this area of your life.

Chapter 8
Talking the Walk

Several years ago while taking a walk through my neighborhood, I passed by the high school football stadium, where a young man was watering the field. When he looked my way, I said, "Hi, how are you doing?"

He routinely replied, "I am doing okay." We then shared some small talk. He told me he was a college student. He went on to say that he liked high school better than young adulthood because life was easier and didn't require so many decisions. He indicated that he was confused about what to do with his life.

At about that time, I could sense the Holy Spirit indicating that this encounter was no mere coincidence but a "divine appointment." I said to the young man: "You know, life doesn't have to be so scary and confusing. God does have a purpose and plan for you."

He rolled his eyes at me and said with a slight laugh: "Yeah, that's what my old girlfriend said to me too. She was some sort of 'Christian,' always talking to me about God and trying to get me into God. I broke up with her!"

"Well, she was right," I interjected. "God does have a special purpose for your life."

"Yeah, and now I'm dating this new chick, and she's saying the same stuff. She's into God too," he voiced with disgust.

"Interesting," I said. "Don't you find it peculiar that you have back-to-back girlfriends who are trying to tell you that God is interested in your life? Now some stranger comes by and tells you the exact same thing they have both been trying to say to you. What do you think are the chances of that?"

He didn't say anything, but he gave me a "that's weird" look.

I continued: "You are fearful, confused, and struggling with what to do with your life, and God hears you. God sent two girls and a stranger to tell you to open your life to him, and God will guide you. God is no doubt trying to get your attention. God engineered this moment because he loves you and wants to be a part of your life."

At this point he had that deer-in-the-headlights look. With his voice trailing, he muttered, "Wow."

"Now quit running from God, and go back to your girlfriend and ask her how you can have a relationship with Christ," I said. Knowing my job was done, I concluded, "I'll be praying for you."

I am not entirely certain what happened to that young man, but I know that the Lord was making an orchestrated effort to reach him with God's love. This student left our encounter pretty intrigued, and I suspect that he had an interesting follow-up conversation with his girlfriend. I was grateful to the Lord for the opportunity to be a part of the Holy Spirit's efforts to communicate God's pursuing love for this young man. In some ways divine coincidences like this make following the Lord a fun adventure.

The fifth characteristic of positively dangerous faith is being a person who is "on evangelistic call" with the Holy

Spirit. We want to live our life in such a way that the Spirit can use us at any time for the purpose of building God's Kingdom. We are about God's business 24/7. Meeting this young man at that football field was nothing unusual or extraordinary. When we are on call, such an encounter is pretty routine.

Jesus Is "On Call"

Jesus is "on call" with the Father and ministers to others as the Father directs him. However, Jesus—led by the Father—evangelizes and ministers in both an intentional and a spontaneous manner. Being on call does not mean that we go about our business until we get "beeped" by the Holy Spirit. Anyone who is on call is also working his or her scheduled hours on the job. We need to be both strategic (seeking ways to share with others) and spontaneous (open to opportunities that present themselves) in our efforts to share the Gospel with others. The key is to be open and genuine in both approaches.

No Evangelization, No Positive Danger

Nothing is positively dangerous about us if we are not sharing with others our relationship with Jesus. We may intrigue others by our love for God and for people. They may be drawn to us because of our authenticity, even respect us because of our integrity. But without effectively communicating the Gospel and inviting others to experience what we have, we are not positively dangerous. Unless we are evangelizers, no one is at risk of catching our faith (see Romans 10:14–15). When it comes to sharing our faith verbally, we must not fall into the "Arctic River Syndrome"—frozen at the mouth! We must *both* "walk the talk" and "talk the walk" to make a maximum impact. Pope Paul VI cautions us about only "walking the talk":

> Nevertheless, this always remains insufficient, because even the finest witness will prove ineffective in the long

run if it is not explained, justified—what Peter called always having "your answer ready for people who ask you the reason for the hope that you all have" (1 Peter 3:15)—and made explicit by a clear and unequivocal proclamation of the Lord Jesus. The Good News proclaimed by the witness of life sooner or later has to be proclaimed by the word of life. There is no true evangelization if the name, the teaching, the life, the promises, the kingdom, and the mystery of Jesus of Nazareth, the Son of God, are not proclaimed.

(*Evangelization in the Modern World,* no. 22)

As Catholics, we understand the importance of such things as liturgy and sacraments, which are a significant part of our Catholic identity and spirituality. Many of us, however, have yet to integrate into our Catholic spirituality the call to share our faith, that is, to *evangelize.* Evangelization is both the essential mission of the Church and our essential responsibility that comes via Baptism. Evangelization is as Catholic as going to Mass on Sunday. Jesus calls us to preach the Gospel to all creation and to make disciples of all nations (see Matthew 28:19, Mark 16:15).

Jesus' Motivation to Evangelize

Jesus never calls us to do something for which he is not a perfect example. Jesus is an evangelizer, and we can learn so much by studying his approach to interpersonal evangelization. The first thing we can learn from Jesus is the proper motivation for evangelizing others. Many religious leaders in his day see no value in reaching people who have no relationship with God. As a matter of fact, they are very critical of Jesus for associating with sinners (see Luke 15:2).

Sometimes Church people today can be this way as well. I've heard many people who regularly attend Mass bitterly complain about losing their customary places on Christmas and Easter on account of the "Chreasters." We can view people as sinners to be avoided instead of souls to be loved. We can get disgusted with the sinner instead of disliking only the sin.

Jesus addresses his religious critics by telling not one but three stories of something lost (see Luke 15:3–32). He tells of a shepherd who leaves ninety-nine sheep and goes in search of the one wanderer. He speaks of a woman who loses one of her ten silver coins and does some serious spring cleaning until she finds it. Jesus describes a son who leaves his father and family in search of the good life, only to find emptiness and despair. The father longs for his son, scanning the horizon daily in search of him. Later the son realizes what he left behind and comes home. The father is so overjoyed by his lost son's return that he calls a big-time party to celebrate. Common to each case—the sheep, the coin, and the son—is the huge party that takes place once they are found.

Jesus obviously overemphasizes the point. He doesn't economize his words: he wants to make himself very clear to his religious critics. He wants them to know without a doubt that people profoundly matter to God. People are deeply loved by God—so much so that we should gladly go out of our way to lead them home. Jesus seeks out sinners, nonreligious people, and societal outcasts because he values them, and so should we. We evangelize because a person is worth more to God than anything. We must learn to see beyond the attitude, the sinfulness, the stench, and the selfishness—seeing instead a beloved soul for whom Jesus died. Because people matter to God, they should matter to us.

Build a Genuine Relationship with Others

Jesus is for people. His very coming into this world is for the purpose of loving people. The incarnation—God's becoming flesh in Jesus—is God's way of walking with us. Jesus enters our world and becomes one of us. He becomes a person in order to reach people.

Furthermore, Jesus builds genuine relationships with those he is seeking to reach. Jesus demonstrates his friendship with Zacchaeus by ignoring the disapproval of the religious leaders and sharing a meal with him and his raunchy friends. Jesus builds a relationship with the Samaritan woman by ignoring cultural taboos and common prejudice. Jesus is relational. He knows that friendship is the sturdiest bridge to another's heart. He understands that by treating others with respect and dignity, he will win a hearing. He recognizes that his genuine concern will provide the credibility needed for others to trust his intentions.

Like Jesus, we must be willing to build genuine relationships with people who will not care about our message until we authentically care for them. Building good relationships means leaving our own agenda and focusing on the life of others. Too often we consider evangelization to be primarily about talking. In reality it's about listening. Without listening we will lack the ability to understand the person with whom we are seeking to share our Good News. Unless we understand people, we will not be able to share the strand of the Gospel that best addresses their spiritual hunger.

Share the Good News in Light of Spiritual Hunger

Jesus is not a "one size fits all" evangelizer. He doesn't share the same message with everyone he is seeking to evangelize. By engaging people and relying on the Holy Spirit's guidance, he spiritually diagnoses those he is attempting to reach. Let's compare two interpersonal, evangelistic encounters that Jesus experiences.

Zacchaeus as a Person (See Luke 19:1–10)

As a tax collector, Zacchaeus is not popular among his fellow Jews, yet his position makes him powerful and wealthy. The Scriptures make note of his small stature; maybe Zacchaeus has a Napoleonic, or short person's, complex and feels some degree of inferiority or insecurity due to his size. Insecure people sometimes seek positions of power to prove to themselves and others that they are not inferior. If Zacchaeus has sought a way to be powerful and wealthy—motivated at least in part by a sense of insecurity—being a tax collector is a good option. Perhaps he is trying to gain a sense of personal dignity through power and riches.

Jesus' Approach

Jesus initiates the encounter. He honors Zacchaeus by singling him out and acknowledging him in the presence of a hostile crowd. Perhaps Zacchaeus's greatest need is simply to be endorsed by someone. Jesus expresses interest in Zacchaeus by inviting himself to the tax collector's house for dinner. Jesus accepts Zacchaeus for who he is, which disarms Zacchaeus. No other religious leaders treat Zacchaeus as a person.

Zacchaeus's greatest longing is for acceptance, dignity, and love. Jesus senses this need and delivers a message (primarily with actions) that addresses the cravings of Zacchaeus's heart. The result is conversion.

The Samaritan Woman as a Person (See John 4:4–26)

She is at the well at noon and alone—a telltale sign that she is not highly esteemed by her female peers. Society ostracizes her because of her lifestyle; she has passed through a litany of broken marriages and is presently involved in an illicit affair. Her heart hungers to be cherished, loved, and cared for. She has a nagging spiritual thirst but is futilely seeking to quench it by finding the right man. She is thirsty but never satisfied.

Jesus' Approach

Jesus breaks with custom and honors the woman by asking for a drink. Not only is it taboo for a man to speak to a woman alone, but even worse, she is a Samaritan, a hated enemy of the Jews. Most of the attention that men have ever given her is probably based on their selfish desires. Jesus shows respect for her during their conversation.

Jesus uses the well as a powerful image, or metaphor, to illustrate the woman's condition. He offers her living water—a substance to satisfy her restless heart. She is trying to fill a God-shaped hole with this world's relationships, and Jesus offers her the substance that will fulfill her longing.

Jesus relates to the Samaritan woman in a very different manner than he does with Zacchaeus. In each case Jesus diagnoses the greatest need and offers the strand of Good News that best addresses the person's real hunger.

Jesus' style of interpersonal evangelization illustrates an essential evangelistic principle. Instead of using a standard or "canned" approach, we need to identify a person's need and tailor the message to address it. For someone who is lonely, we can present the Gospel as a relationship with Christ, who cares and is the friend of a lonely heart. To another who feels inferior, we can offer Jesus, who has validated our existence by dying for us. His death establishes how valuable we are to the Father. One of our peers may be constantly anxious and worried about life. We can share how our Lord cares so much for us that the hairs on our head are numbered.

The Good News we share must be based on the Scriptures. We do not have the liberty to make up what we think is Good News. If our message is contrary to the Scriptures and to Church teaching, we are in error. It is important, therefore, to know the Scriptures and the teaching of the Church. The Holy Spirit will then be able to draw from our previous deposits during the present time of need (see Mark 13:11).

(This section, pp. 107–109, is adapted from Frank Mercadante, *Growing Teen Disciples,* pp. 149–151.)

Invitation

When I was in sixth grade, my friend Bobby announced to all of us that he was going to have a big birthday party. For the next several weeks, he divulged specific details about this party that quickly elevated its status to "the party of the century." Bobby was breaking new ground by inviting the opposite sex to his party. Up to that time, we all attended single-sex gatherings. Along with all this, it was a sleepover!

However, one small detail that Bobby failed to share with me was driving me crazy as the party date got closer. My entire social status was on the line because of the detail Bobby didn't share with me: Was I invited to Bobby's party of the century? Somehow, because we were friends, Bobby presumed that I would know I was invited.

Sometimes we approach evangelization in the same way. We may share with others how Jesus has made a difference in our life—even share the strand of the Good News that best suits their spiritual hunger—yet fail to invite them to experience Jesus personally. Invitation is the bridge that takes a person from the message of Jesus to the experience of Jesus and provides the transition from the evangelizer's faith experience to the evangelized person's faith experience.

We can invite people by simply asking, "Is there anything standing in the way of making Jesus the most important person in your life?" If there is, we may want to address those barriers. If there is not, we may want to ask if we can pray with these people. Then we can lead them in a short prayer that addresses their most significant spiritual hunger with the appropriate strand of the Gospel. If they are comfortable, we can encourage them to pray in a way that invites Jesus to be more a part of their life.

We should also support their faith growth by inviting them to be a part of our faith community. We should consider the programs in our youth ministry that best address their present spiritual needs. Evangelization is not just about initiating a relationship with Jesus. It is also important to help others become part of a community of faith that can support their growing faith.

Summary

Without sharing our faith with others, we cannot be positively dangerous, which is all about placing others at great risk of catching our faith, about living our life in a manner that attracts others and draws their interest. But if we don't have the ability to share what it is that makes us different, we won't have the ability to be dangerous. Our faith can be contagious only if we share it.

Jesus is the best example of a person who lives "on evangelistic call." He is motivated to share the Gospel with others because he understands the value of a soul and, therefore, makes the most of every evangelistic opportunity. He respects people, treats them with dignity, and builds genuine relationships. Guided by the Spirit, he diagnoses the hunger in each person's heart and explains the Gospel in light of that hunger. By following his example, we too will be positively dangerous.

Conclusion

If there is ever a time when our world needs positively dangerous people, it is now. We need young, jalapeÖo leaders who will be the next generation of saints. Our world hungers for real people of true substance. Fakes, artificial believers, convenience Catholics, and compromisers turn people away from Christ and from the Church. We need an army of positively dangerous youth to live and to share our faith in a fresh, new way that attracts other people to Jesus.

First, being positively dangerous means being a person who has depth. It's about substance, not image. Real substance begins with our relationship with God. Positively dangerous people make their relationship with God their first priority and are learning to love the Lord with all their heart, mind, and strength.

Second, positively dangerous people know how to love other people with abandon by placing others' needs before their own. They communicate love in very practical ways.

Third, positively dangerous people are real, genuine, and authentic. They and their message attract others because of being steeped in commonness, not in arrogance.

Fourth, positively dangerous people walk the talk by living with integrity. The message of the Gospel speaks loudly through their life.

Fifth, positively dangerous people are evangelizers. They rely on the Holy Spirit to help them verbally share the Gospel in both a spontaneous and an intentional manner.

Finally, living in a positively dangerous manner is something you are never meant to do alone. It is best practiced in community. Instead of being just a "lone ranger" who is positively dangerous, seek to be part of a positively dangerous community. To make it over the long haul, you will need the encouragement, support, and challenge of other believers. Collective efforts can once again, like the Apostles before you, turn the world upside down!

Questions for Reflection and Discussion

1. Have you ever had an experience of being on evangelistic call? If so, describe it.

2. What are the most significant obstacles that stand in the way of your being an effective evangelizer?

3. Do you agree or disagree that nothing is positively dangerous about you if you are not sharing with others your relationship with Jesus? Please explain your answer.

4. For many Catholics evangelization is not a primary part of their spirituality. How much is it a part of yours? Please explain your answer.

5. People deeply matter to God, as Jesus illustrates in the parables of the lost sheep, the lost coin, and the prodigal son. What motivates you to reach out to others with the Gospel?

6. Sometimes you can miss evangelistic opportunities. How can you be more alert and aware? In what existing relationships are you in a position to share your faith?

7. What does building genuine relationships with people mean? Why is this context effective in sharing your faith?

8. What are today's most significant spiritual hungers? How are people expressing them? What strands of the Gospel address them?

9. On a scale of one to ten (one is low, and ten is high), how do you rate yourself as a spontaneous evangelizer? as an intentional evangelizer? What practical steps can help you improve in each aspect?

10. If the teens in your youth ministry program were to take evangelization seriously, what impact would they have?

11. If the teens in your youth ministry program were to apply the five characteristics of being positively dangerous, what changes would you see in your youth ministry program?

Acknowledgments (continued from copyright page)

The stories about David, Nicole, and Steven, on pages 10–13; the naive and unemployed young man, on page 35; Becky and Jessica, on pages 65–67, a group of teens at a summer conference, on pages 89–90, and the approach of Jesus to evangelization, on pages 107–109 are adapted from *Growing Teen Disciples: Strategies for Really Effective Youth Ministry,* by Frank Mercadante (Winona, MN: Saint Mary's Press, 2002), pages 244–246, 32–33, 26–27, 31–32, and 149–151, respectively. Copyright © 1998 by Cultivation Ministries. All rights reserved.

The survey of college students referred to on page 18 is from "Why I'm Not a Christian," by Robert M. Kachur, *HIS Magazine,* vol. 46, no. 5, February 1986, page 8.

The story about Karl Marx, on page 19, is adapted from *Give Me an Answer,* by Cliffe Knechtle (Downers Grove, IL: InterVarsity Press, 1986), page 95. Copyright © 1986 by Inter-Varsity Christian Fellowship of the United States of America. All rights reserved.

The story about Telemachus, on pages 24–26, is adapted from *Radically Committed,* by Jim Burns (Dallas: Word Publishing, 1991), pages 44–46. Copyright © 1991 by Jim Burns. All rights reserved. Used with permission of the author.

The story about the Gulf War colonel and the private, on pages 34–35, is taken from *Becoming a Contagious Christian,* by Bill Hybels and Mark Mittelberg (Grand Rapids, MI: Zondervan, 1994), page 57. Copyright © 1994 by Bill Hybels and Mark Mittelberg. All rights reserved. Used with permission of Zondervan.

The story on pages 40–41 about the group of Christian believers in the former Soviet Union is adapted from a tape in the author's possession of a presentation by Larry Tomczak at the Catholic Charismatic Conference, University of Notre Dame, 1978.

The quotation on page 47 is from *Homilies on the First Epistle of John,* by Saint Augustine, no. 7:8.

The quotations from Mother Teresa on pages 54, 55, and 58 are from *Mother Teresa: A Simple Path,* compiled by Lucinda Vardey (New York: Ballantine Books, 1995), pages xi, 7, and 7, respectively. Copyright © 1995 by Mother Teresa. All rights reserved.

The story about the shepherds and their flocks of sheep, on page 55, is adapted from *A Prophetic Vision for the 21st Century: A Spiritual Map to Help You Navigate into the Future,* by Rick Joyner (Nashville, TN: Thomas Nelson Publishers, 1999), page 74. Copyright © 1999 by Rick Joyner. All rights reserved. Used with permission

The quotation on page 63 is from *Total Surrender,* by Mother Teresa, edited by Br. Angelo Devananda Scolozzi, pages 35–36. Copyright © 1985 by Missionaries of Charity; selections and arrangement of material copyright © 1985 by Br. Angelo Devananda Scolozzi. Published by Servant Publications (www.servantpub.com), P.O. Box 8617, Ann Arbor, Michigan, 48107. Used with permission.

The story about the boy frightened by a thunderstorm, on page 68, is from *If I Were Starting My Family Again,* by John Drescher (Nashville, TN: Abingdon, 1979), page 62. Copyright © 1979 by Abingdon. All rights reserved.

The portion of words to the song "Thank You," by Ray Boltz, quoted on page 70, is from the CD *Moments for the Heart: The Very Best of Ray Boltz;* "Thank You" words and music copyright © 1988 by Gaither Music Company. All rights controlled by Gaither Copyright Management. Used with permission.

The quotation from Ralph Waldo Emerson on page 91 is from "Social Aims," in *Letters and Social Aims* (Boston: Houghton Mifflin, 1917), page 96. Copyright © 1917 by Edward W. Emerson. All rights reserved.

The story about the Great Blondin, on page 98, is adapted from *Small Group Leader's Guide for Teens,* by Frank Mercadante (Washington, DC: Paulist National Catholic Evangelization Association, 1999), pages 8–9. Copyright © 1999 by the Paulist National Catholic Evangelization Association. All rights reserved.

The quotation from Pope Paul VI on pages 104–105 is from Apostolic Exhortation *Evangelii Nuntiandi (Evangelization in the Modern World),* no. 22, accessed at *www.vatican.va/holy_father/ paul_vi/apost_exhortations/ documents/hf_p-vi_exh_19751208_evangelii-nuntiandi_en.html,* April 22, 2003.

To review copyright terms and conditions for the Internet material cited here, log on to the home page for the referenced Web site.

During this book's preparation, all citations, facts, figures, names, addresses, telephone numbers, Internet URLs, and other information cited within were verified for accuracy. The author and Saint Mary's Press staff have made every attempt to reference current and valid sources, but we cannot guarantee the content of any source, and we are not responsible for any changes that may have occurred since our verification. If you find an error in, or have a question or concern about, any of the information or sources listed within, please contact Saint Mary's Press.